Classic Pathfinder 4

Doing it for themselves

Classic
PATHFINDER

You speak, they speak: focus on target language use
(CLASSIC PATHFINDER 1)
Barry Jones, Susan Halliwell and Bernardette Holmes

Challenging classes: focus on pupil behaviour
(CLASSIC PATHFINDER 2)
Jenifer Alison and Susan Halliwell

Inspiring performance: focus on drama and song
(CLASSIC PATHFINDER 3)
Judith Hamilton, Anne McLeod and Steven Fawkes

CILT, the National Centre for Languages, seeks to support and develop multilingualism and intercultural competence among all sectors of the population in the UK.

CILT is a registered charity, supported by Central Government grants.

Classic
PATHFINDER

4

Doing it for themselves: focus on learning strategies and vocabulary building

VEE HARRIS & DAVID SNOW

CiLT The National Centre for Languages

The views expressed in this publication are the authors' and do not necessarily represent those of CILT, the National Centre for Languages

First published 2004 by CILT, the National Centre for Languages, 20 Bedfordbury, London WC2N 4LB

Printed in Great Britain by Hobbs

CILT Publications are available from: **Central Books**, 99 Wallis Rd, London E9 5LN. Tel: 0845 458 9910. Fax: 0845 458 9912. Book trade representation (UK and Ireland): **Broadcast Book Services**, Charter House, 29a London Rd, Croydon CR0 2RE. Tel: 020 8681 8949. Fax: 020 8688 0615.

Contents

Foreword

This book constitutes further thoughts on two particularly pertinent aspects of language learning in the light of developments over recent years. The focus is essentially on how teachers can show learners how they can learn better, be that in skills development, concept development, or development of learning processes and techniques. Strategy training for pupils together with vocabulary building is an important element of the *Key Stage 3 Framework for MFL* and this publication will be very useful to teachers in implementing the Strategy in England. But there is much else besides. The authors take a detailed and thought-provoking approach, showing how learning strategies are essential to the developing language learner.

By 1997, Vee Harris had begun to explore in concrete terms how, in order to become autonomous of their teachers, pupils needed to learn **how** to learn a foreign language. The result was Pathfinder 31: *Teaching learners how to learn* in which she reported on work with local schools and her PGCE students at Goldsmiths College, putting together some ideas which were generalisable to other classrooms. In that book she discussed her initial plans for a 'strategy training cycle'. These ideas have proved influential over the ensuing years. Since that time she has worked with many European colleagues to extend the notion of strategy training, engaging in research and co-publishing, with Mike Grenfell, the excellent book, *Modern Languages and learning strategies: In theory and practice.*

The second part of the book focuses on building vocabulary. In it David Snow demonstrates in a very practical way techniques and strategies that language learners need to develop in order to become independent of their teachers. His ideas are at the same time very appealing, challenging and engaging for teachers and learners alike.

The literature on ways of teaching pupils how to learn has multiplied since the time these two *Pathfinders* were written. In this *Classic Pathfinder* the authors have revisited substantially the original publications. This is not so much a re-edition as a digest of further thoughts.

Ann Swarbrick
Head of Professional Advice, CILT

Part 1

Teaching learners how to learn

Strategy training in the MFL classroom

VEE HARRIS

Acknowledgements

This book would not have been possible without the hard work, energy and initiative of the teachers and student teachers I have had the privilege of working with. In the original edition, Pathfinder 31: *Teaching learners how to learn*, I acknowledged the enormous contribution of the following teachers who completed the CILT/Goldsmiths MA module on 'Learning strategies': Angelina Adams, Marian Carty, Pamela Dewey, Jacqueline Footman and Fiona Lunskey.

To these names, I need now to add those of former student teachers from the Goldsmiths Modern Languages PGCE whose imaginative material is included in this revised edition:

Katrin Artz, Mim Bowker, Lindsey Hand, Pamela Harkness, Natalie Mendes and Augusta Viera, Cheryl Michael and Heather Wright.

I am also indebted to the following teachers who are currently working with me on the pilot study of the STIR Project (STrategy Instruction Research) for their insightful comments on how their pupils learn: Fiona Lunskey, Maureen Oswald, Jennie Prescott and Kate Scappaticci.

I would also like to thank Ann Swarbrick (CILT), who first showed me the Dutch poem, and Bernardette Holmes and Emma Rees (CILT) for the painstaking comments they made on the initial drafts of this edition. Finally, I want to thank my daughter Sophie for providing the illustrations on pages 22 and 26.

Introduction

In the first edition of this book, Pathfinder 31: *Teaching learners how to learn* (1997), I expressed concern that the drive to 'raise achievement' may have left Modern Languages teachers feeling that they should be drawing yet more colourful flashcards or devising further sets of differentiated worksheets. I suggested that an alternative approach was to focus on enabling the pupils to become more effective learners. In that way, the responsibility for their progress could be shared between pupils and teacher.

Since 1997, we have seen a revised National Curriculum for Modern Foreign Languages (DfEE 1999), Optional Schemes of Work for MFL (DfEE 2000), Curriculum 2000 (QCA 1999) and now the various initiatives involved in the Key Stage 3 National Strategy. At first sight, these changes appear to face teachers with yet more new challenges. However, on closer examination, making explicit how to learn emerges as a common theme across all these developments, so that it is even more relevant today than in 1997. One of the key principles of the *Key Stage 3 MFL Framework* (DfES 2003a: 12), for example, is to:

Principle	Action
Build reflection	Teach pupils to think about what and how they learn and involve them in setting targets for future lessons

The *KS3 MFL Framework* invites us to use plenaries at the end of the lesson as a key opportunity to engage pupils in such reflection. The value of teaching pupils the strategies they need to function more effectively on their own is also reflected in:

- the objectives of the Framework. These are structured to build up from a 'firm foundation' in Year 7, through 'acceleration' in Year 8, towards 'pupils' independence as language learners' in Year 9. (Examples of how the objectives relate to learning strategies can be found in Chapter 1);
- 'The reflection challenge' which is a key constituent of the Key Stage 3 'Learning challenge' units (DfES 2003b). These are designed to provide 'catch-up' intervention for pupils performing below expectation for their age;
- the 'Teaching and Learning in Secondary Schools' pilot self-study units (DfES 2003c). Unit 8, for example, is devoted to the theme of developing effective learners.

Given this common emphasis at KS3, it seems likely that any further changes to be made in the 14–19 curriculum will build on the assumption that pupils have been taught to become effective and independent language learners. So far from being yet one more pressure on Modern Languages teachers, teaching pupils how to learn can help us address some of the new initiatives we are faced with.

It can also help address some of our long-standing concerns. The issue of differentiation has become even more pressing with our growing understanding of research into different learning styles (Gardner 1993). Some learners like to have a written text in front of them; it is a kind of 'prop', even if the aims of the activity are oral. Others are happier in the oral/aural mode; they like to listen to and speak the language, undistracted by the written word. Some learners like to be told grammatical rules, others find them confusing. They prefer to work out the rules for themselves, sometimes unconsciously, by listening to the language, reading it and trying to use it. We can and should create differentiated tasks for our pupils, but this is time-consuming and at best we may only offer a choice of three or four different activities. But the problem can be tackled from another angle – one which recognises that learning is unique to each individual. By actively helping pupils to discover the most useful ways for them to learn, we can enable them to make the best use of the learning opportunities offered both within and outside the classroom.

Boys' underachievement in Modern Foreign Languages has continued to be a source of concern over the five years since the publication of Pathfinder 31. However, recent research (Jones and Jones 2001) reinforces the importance of:

- giving a clear and explicit reason for all the activities which the teacher organises so that pupils understand how these activities are going to help them learn;
- giving pupils more 'ownership', not only in the choice of content but also how they go about their learning.

Similarly, Graham and Rees (1995) stress how a better understanding of the learning process can help address some of the disaffection we face in the classroom:

> If pupils are helped to perceive a link between the strategies employed and the resulting outcomes, however, their sense of control over their own learning could be heightened and a powerful source of motivation harnessed.

Beyond these immediate considerations, it is interesting to see that within the research literature on learning strategies, the past five years have also seen an increasing emphasis on 'learner self-management' (Rubin 2001). The shift is away from just teaching pupils the particular strategies they need to tackle a reading task, for example, or memorise a list of vocabulary. It has moved to a more general concern to enable pupils to become aware of their own approach to language learning and to take a more active role in choosing for themselves which strategies they will use for any task and how they will evaluate the outcomes.

So in preparing this new edition, my aim has been to:

- take account of the most recent research into learning strategies;
- provide clear links to the KS3 Strategy and other Government initiatives.

In addition, this new edition:

- gives examples of how to teach listening and writing strategies, as well as the memorisation and reading strategies which were illustrated in the original *Pathfinder 31*. The intervening years have allowed me to share more ideas with teachers, and student teachers, and some of their classroom experiences and materials are a new feature of the book;
- gives greater guidance on 'which strategies to teach when', as this is an issue that has been frequently raised in INSET sessions that I have run;
- makes the lists of strategies more 'pupil friendly' and integrates them into the chapters which describe how to teach them.

You will find photocopiable strategy checklists in the following chapters:

Chapter	Strategy checklist
2	Strategies for memorising vocabulary and grammar and collaborative strategies for working in groups
3	Strategies for reading, writing and checking written work
4	Listening strategies
5	Speaking strategies

You may want to use the checklists to:

- add strategies you yourself used as a learner when you were in school;
- tick strategies your pupils already use;
- cross strategies they do not use but which you would like them to;
- ask pupils to tick the strategies they already use;
- ask pupils to tick the strategies they could use to extend their repertoire.

Traditionally, we tend to feel we should read books from start to finish. The intention here is that you, the reader, start with the chapter that you feel would be most useful for you and then, if you are interested and want more information, you proceed to another chapter. We suggest, however, that everyone starts by reading Chapters 1 and 2.

1 What are learning strategies and how can they help us?

WHAT ARE LEARNING STRATEGIES?

As MFL teachers, it is particularly hard for us to know what language learning strategies are, as by definition, we are successful linguists. So when we were learning a new language in school, we often used these strategies automatically, without even being aware of them.

To gain some insight into these strategies, it may be helpful to put yourself in the situation of tackling a new language again. Start by translating as much as you can of the following Dutch text:

Een appel is rood,
de zon is geel,
de hemel is blauw,
een blad is groen,
een wolk is wit …
en de aarde is bruin.

En zou je nu kunnen
antwoorden
op de vraag …
welke kleur de liefde heeft

from *Welke kleur heeft de liefde?* by Joan Walsh Anglund (Zomer & Keuning, Wageningen, Holland)

Given that MFL teachers are usually interested in the way any new language operates, it is likely that you managed to work out the meaning of most of the poem, although the last sentences may have caused some difficulties, since they are particularly dependent on some knowledge of grammar.

Now try to list what you did to work out the meaning of a poem in a completely unfamiliar language.

It is likely that the strategies you used included some of the following:

- recognising the type of text (in this case, a poem from a child's book) and therefore having some expectations of what it might be about, its overall structure, etc;
- looking for cognates (words that look or sound familiar through knowledge of English, French, German, Spanish, etc);
- using the pattern of the sentences to predict meaning ('a something is + colour');
- using common sense and knowledge of the world. Although the author could be engaged in a flight of poetic fancy and creating an imaginary world, once we have established that she is referring to the colours of the natural environment, we can make a safe guess as to the colour of the sun, clouds etc;
- saying the text out loud;
- using the pictures (although not everyone notices the little drawings behind the children).

Furthermore, as successful language learners, you probably used these strategies not one by one but in combination, so that as you read you kept checking back to see if your first guesses were correct.

These kinds of strategies are obviously very helpful in enabling us to tackle a new language, so why not let pupils in on the secret and make our own knowledge explicit? As Rubin (1990: 282) points out:

> *Often poorer learners don't have a clue as to how good learners arrive at their answers and feel that they can never perform as good learners do. By revealing the process, this myth can be exposed.*

If you want to find out what other strategies successful language learners have in their repertoire, use yourself as a good example before reading the next chapters. What did you do to learn either your first foreign language or your second? You may find it interesting to compare the strategies you identify to the checklists of strategies in the appropriate chapter. Which ones are you already using? Are there any that you do not use? Why? What does it tell you about your preferred learning style?

- How did you memorise vocabulary? (see Chapter 2)
- How did you memorise grammar rules? (see Chapter 2)
- How did you go about writing a text and then checking it? (see Chapter 3)
- What did you do when listening to a radio programme or a tape and there was something you did not immediately understand? (see Chapter 4)

- What did you do when you had something to say but did not know the precise word (see Chapter 5)?

You may also want to compare your strategies to the strategies you think your pupils use. Do successful pupils use more than the unsuccessful ones? Do advanced pupils have a wider repertoire?

WHY TEACH LEARNING STRATEGIES?

The evidence is complex, but research (O'Malley and Chamot 1990) suggests that some strategies may be easier than others and hence acquired earlier. These are the strategies used by low attainers and tend to be at a fairly simple level. It appears that these learners fail to move on to develop the more complex strategies used by successful language learners. Effective learners in both the reading and listening skill areas, for example, seem to use both a 'top-down' and a 'bottom-up' approach. In other words, they know how to identify the general gist of the text, to attack it at a global level, as well as how to perform 'word-for-word' literal translation and analysis where necessary. Low attainers, on the other hand, seem to be limited to the 'bottom-up' approach to comprehension. They try to translate each word and often rapidly become disheartened when they do not know its meaning. Not only is their range narrower, but they also seem to use strategies less frequently and to have problems in knowing which strategies to use when. Johnstone (1993) in his study of Scottish primary school pupils learning Modern Languages notes that, whereas the class as a whole may identify fourteen to fifteen strategies, each individual pupil may be using only two or three. The question then arises as to whether the teacher should simply accept pupils' limitations as inevitable or whether to intervene and set about teaching them the strategies they are lacking.

In fact, a number of learning strategies are included in the list of skills in the National Curriculum Programme of Study Part 1 that 'pupils should be taught' (DfEE 1999). They range from what could be described as basic study skills like using a dictionary (3d) or acquiring 'techniques for memorising words, phrases and short extracts' (3a), to more complex skills like 'how to use context and other clues to interpret meaning' (3b) or to 'redraft their writing to improve its accuracy and presentation'(2j) .

The *KS3 MFL Framework* gives further weight to the value of explicitly teaching these strategies. The left-hand column of the table below lists some of the strategies that pupils should be taught at Year 7. These are not just useful strategies for MFL learning, however, but also for developing pupils' English. In the right-hand column, you will see a comparison to similar strategies advocated either in the *KS3 Framework for Teaching English* (DfES 2001b) or in the National Literacy Strategy (DfES 1998).

 **KS3 MFL Framework**	 **The teaching of English**
Pupils should be taught ...	*Pupils should be taught ...*
how to find and **memorise** the spelling, sound, meaning and main attributes of words (p45)	to identify words which pose a particular challenge and learn them by using mnemonics, multi-sensory reinforcement and memorising critical features (*Framework for Teaching English*: 23)
how to **read** and understand simple texts using cues in language, layout and context to aid understanding (p51)	to use titles, cover pages, pictures to predict the content of unfamiliar stories (*National Literacy Strategy*: 24)
how to evaluate and improve the quality of their **written** work (p36)	to re-read own writing to check for grammatical sense (coherence) and accuracy (agreement) – identify errors and suggest alternative constructions (*National Literacy Strategy*: 28)
how to extend, link and develop sentences to form continuous text (p37)	to develop ways of linking paragraphs, using a range of strategies to improve cohesion and coherence, e.g. choice of connectives, reference back, linking phrases (*Framework for Teaching English*: 26)
skills they need when **listening** to the media (p37) to begin to interpret what they hear from content and tone and listen for inferences (p38)	to recognise the way familiar spoken texts e.g. directions, explanations, are organised and identify their typical features, e.g. of vocabulary or tone (*Framework for Teaching English*: 24)
how to use a **dictionary** and other resources appropriately when working on a text (p36)	to use the quartiles of a dictionary and find words beyond the initial letter (*Framework for Teaching English*: 23)

It is interesting to note that pupils entering Year 7 at level 3 or below encounter strategies again, since the KS3 'catch-up' Progress Units (DfES 2001a) include materials designed to explicitly teach memorisation and reading strategies.

We cannot assume, however, that without our help, pupils will automatically transfer the strategies from one language to another. With a small team of teachers from London schools, I have been working on a research project to explore whether pupils are already making the links between their English and MFL learning. There seems to be some suggestion that while high attainers appear to see the common ground, others perceive the languages as existing in entirely separate boxes.

So without ignoring what is unique to Modern Languages, it may be helpful to make explicit to pupils that many strategies can be transferred between languages. Primary school pupils may be particularly receptive since the struggle to learn to read, for example, may still be fresh in their minds.

Such a cross-curricular approach to teaching strategies could enable pupils to develop:

- memorisation skills such as 'look-cover-test-check' which apply to information recall in any subject area;
- reading strategies to help them tackle the dense and complex texts they sometimes encounter in History, Science or Geography;
- drafting and redrafting strategies using ICT;
- dictionary skills, relevant to English as well as MFL;
- study skills, such as note-taking or revising, in lessons such as PSHE.

A further argument for this approach emerges from the research literature. Studies into English (see Harrison 2002 for a review) and into foreign language learning (Cohen 1998, Rubin 1990) highlight the importance of extensive practice in the deployment of strategies if they are to be effectively internalised. So it seems likely that having two contexts rather than one in which pupils can activate their language-learning strategies can only be beneficial. For a fuller discussion of the potential value of MFL and English teachers working together see Harris and Grenfell (forthcoming).

Over and above developing specific language-learning skills, offering pupils insights into the learning process and how best they as individuals learn allows them to take a more equal role in their own education and to develop as confident, independent learners. It can equip them with tools that they will be able to use long after they leave school.

The past fifteen years have been marked by an increasing interest in learner autonomy (Dickinson 1987; Holec 1988; Little 1991). As Nunan (1995: 134) points out, however:

> *It is a mistake to assume that learners come into the language classroom with*
> *a natural ability to make choices about what and how to learn.*

This first became evident to me some ten years ago when I started to work with a group of London teachers to explore how to take the initial steps away from a teacher-centred classroom. We gradually began to be aware of a range of problems (Grenfell and Harris 1993). Many of the pupils did not know how to use a dictionary. They were reduced to panic when faced with reading authentic material without the teacher's support and some of them lacked the basic social skills to support each other in group work. It seemed that for autonomy to work, it was not enough to organise the classroom in such a way that a range of resources and activities were on offer. Pupils had to be taught the skills and strategies they needed to tackle things on their own. Only in that way could they be expected to make the most of the opportunities offered them.

What appears to be of key importance in the process is not just to teach pupils the specific 'cognitive' strategies they need to tackle a particular skill area, but more generally to help them to develop the global, overarching 'metacognitive' strategies that successful, independent learners use to reflect on and take control of their learning. Rubin (2001) sees 'learner self management' as a vital tool in developing pupils' independence, since it enables them:

- to plan how they will tackle any task in whatever skill area;
- to monitor how well they are doing it;
- to evaluate how successfully they have done it.

The Common European Framework of Reference for Learning, Teaching and Assessment of Modern Languages (1996) also emphasises the importance of these higher-level, general, metacognitive strategies, by grouping the cognitive strategies under the four main categories of:

- planning;
- execution;
- evaluation;
- repair.

Since these metacognitive strategies can seem somewhat abstract, some concrete examples are provided in the table overleaf in relation to writing. The examples are grouped under:

- '**before** writing' (*planning*);
- '**while** writing' (*monitoring*);
- '**after** writing' (*evaluating*).

You will find a more detailed checklist of writing strategies in Chapter 3.

The next chapter considers how we can teach pupils these metacognitive strategies alongside the more skill-specific strategies. To highlight their importance, the cognitive strategies involved in each skill area are again listed under the headings of:

- before;
- while;
- after.

Clearly, this kind of reflection on and control over their own learning is part and parcel of the 'thinking skills' discussed in New Pathfinder 4: *It makes you think! Creating engagement, offering challenges* (Jones and Swarbrick 2004). In this publication, the authors consider what teachers can do to ensure that pupils think for themselves in their language lessons. They discuss how, if we revisit some commonly used teaching techniques, we can make them at once more demanding of pupils and more challenging.

Before writing (*Planning*)	**Example**
I have thought about the working conditions that suit me best in order to complete the task	I need to do this homework in a quiet room/after I have talked it through with my friend.
I have looked at the task and identified what is required	I will read over exactly what we have to do; how long does the letter have to be? What points do I need to cover in it?
I have decided how I am going to tackle it	I will start by trying to think of all the things I could say. Then I will look for more ideas and some useful words and expressions in my book/the coursebook.
I have thought about what to concentrate on	When I start writing, I am not going to worry about getting my tenses right; I'll just get my ideas down on paper. Then I'll come back and check what I have written.
I have identified any problems and thought about ways to resolve them, e.g. using a dictionary, asking a friend/ the teacher	I won't be able to finish this letter because I don't know how to say 'Yours sincerely'. I will look it up in the dictionary.

While writing (*Monitoring*)	
I can keep myself going even when I encounter difficulties	I don't know how to say this and I can't find it in the dictionary. That's all right. I'll do the next few sentences and see if that helps. Sometimes coming back to something difficult later seems to leave your brain time to work on finding a way round it.
I have tracked how well my chosen strategies are working and revised them if necessary	I thought I could do this letter just by using the ideas in my head, but I think I need to look at examples of letters in the coursebook. One of my targets was to check my spelling as I went along. I think I am doing OK.

After writing (*Evaluating*)	
I check back to see if it makes sense or I have made a grammatical mistake	I've missed out a word here. I need to make the adjective agree with the subject.
I know what I have successfully grasped and what I still need to work on	I have managed to write a simple letter, but I need to look now at how to 'make it fancy' so I can reach Level 6.

2 Principles of strategy instruction: Memorisation and collaborative strategies

The most important principles of strategy instruction are to go about it systematically, over a length of time and linked to the everyday tasks pupils face in the classroom. It cannot be undertaken as a 'one-off' lesson or covered only in PSHE periods. Pupils need to apply the strategies directly to Modern Languages tasks and to practise them extensively. Most writers on strategy instruction advocate a sequence of similar steps or stages (for a comparison of various researchers' sequences of steps, see Harris 2003). Chapter 3 gives some detailed examples of what these steps look like for reading and writing strategies and for strategies for checking work. It might be useful first to summarise the stages briefly in relation to the teaching of memorisation strategies, so that the principles behind each step are clear. I have chosen memorisation strategies as in many ways they are the easiest to teach. The question of which strategies to teach when is discussed in more detail in Chapter 4.

As you read through the cycle of steps, you may notice that steps two, four and five are very similar to the sequence of presentation, practice and production used to teach the language of a new topic. Whether learning new language, new concepts or new strategies, pupils need the teacher's support to enable them to move from understanding to independent use. Based on Vygotsky's work (1962, 1978) the notion of 'scaffolding' pupils' learning in this way is increasingly recognised as essential across all subjects in the curriculum.

THE CYCLE OF STRATEGY INSTRUCTION: MEMORISATION STRATEGIES

Beginning teachers often devote hours to planning a lesson, then finally remember that it is 'homework night' and decide that it will simply have to be to 'learn the vocabulary'. I became particularly interested in this when I noticed that my son assured me that he was 'doing his homework', when in fact he was mindlessly copying down words, as he watched 'Neighbours' on television! What was he learning and how? This made me aware that we cannot maximise the opportunities independent study provides unless we provide clear guidelines on how to learn.

Step 1	Step 2	Step 3	Step 4	Step 5
Awareness raising	Modelling	Action planning	Extensive practice and Fading out the reminders	Evaluation

Step 1: Awareness raising

The first step in the strategy instruction cycle is aimed at making pupils think about the strategies they already use. Set them a familiar task 'cold' – in other words without mentioning anything about strategies, for example 'learn these ten words for homework'. Then, in the next lesson ask them how they went about it, while it is still fresh in their minds.

How can I learn my French vocabulary?!

Read through these *learning strategies* to help you improve your language learning.
Tick the boxes and keep trying new ways to learn!

nouns   verbs   adjectives   adverbs   articles   prepositions   etc

LEARNING STRATEGY	TRIED IT	IT HELPS
1. write out list of words in French with the English alongside, and keep copying out the French till I know them without looking back		
2. test myself by covering up either the French or English		
3. get someone else (friend/brother/sister/parent/etc.) to test me		
4. chant the words out loud		
5. mime the words as I say them, in front of the mirror		
6. mime the words with a friend, each one has to guess		
7. put the words to a familiar tune or song		
8. make up a song or poem with the new words		
9. make up quizzes or puzzles for a friend or for me to do later (word searches, crosswords, anagrams, etc.)		
10. play Hangman or other games with someone to practise		
11. draw pictures to illustrate the words, then cover up the word and write it, using the pictures as prompts		
12. add different words into familiar sentences		
13. write the words on labels to stick around the house – in the bedroom, kitchen, bathroom, lounge, etc.		
14. read through the words just before going to bed at night, and just after waking up in the morning		
15. brainstorm words on a particular topic, looking up any extra words, and checking the spellings of others in a dictionary		
16. write down a list of words, then write down all the opposites for them, or a related word		
17. teach someone else the new words		
18. tape words and listen to them while getting dressed/washing up/tidying your room etc.		
19. separate the **articles** (*le, la, les, l'*) and words, and match them up again. Colour-code the cards to help you.		
20. to learn the **accents**, put the accents on Post-It notes, write the words out on bits of paper, and add the right Post-It, checking the words afterwards.		

The more strategies you can use, the better you will learn, and the more fun and interesting it will be. Some are: -

	visual strategies	learn by *looking*
	auditory strategies	learn by *listening*
	kinaesthetic strategies	learn by *doing*
	tactile strategies	learn by *feeling*
	individual strategies	learn *on your own*
	group strategies	learn *with others*

Brainstorm the strategies they used and collect the ideas on the board. Now explain that the aim is to widen their repertoire of strategies. At this point, it is vital to persuade the class of the value of trying out new strategies. High attainers may need to be reminded not to become complacent and that, although they are making progress, they might improve even further (or simply find the work easier) if they adopt new strategies. Low attainers, who believe they are 'no good at languages', may need convincing that the problems they have experienced so far with learning the language may be due to lack of strategies, rather than lack of ability. The brainstorming can also lead into a useful discussion of different learning styles; do they prefer to write down words (visual learners) or say them aloud (auditory learners), for example? In the checklist of memorisation strategies that a student teacher, Mim Bowker, used (opposite), you might want to indicate next to each strategy the kind of learning style it suits.

You will find plenty of other ideas for learning vocabulary in Part 2 of this book, *Words: Teaching and learning vocabulary*. Look out for the difference between activities that **you the teacher** could do and those that **the pupils** could do themselves at home to help them learn their vocabulary independently.

Step 2: Modelling

In the course of discussing how they went about memorising the words for homework, pupils themselves can make excellent teachers, explaining to the rest of the class the strategies that work for them. But there are likely to be some strategies that no one mentions that you know are helpful. For example, 'thinking of an English word that sounds vaguely like the word you are trying to learn'. I remember the Swahili word for giraffe (*twiga*) by thinking that the giraffe's legs look like twigs. Pamela Dewey (one of the teachers whose work was drawn on in Pathfinder 31) gives a good example of a pupil who thought of keys (*clés*) made of clay. We often tell pupils these kinds of tips for remembering a particular word. But they need to know **how** we worked out that tip in the first place. So this step is about 'modelling' new strategies, making it clear exactly how to go about them. 'Thinking aloud' has long been part and parcel of the learning strategies research literature as a way of 'letting pupils in on the secret'. It is now also advocated as one of the cross-curriculum principles in the Key Stage 3 Strategy as a vital way of 'making concepts and conventions explicit'. You can see a teacher using it to model reading strategies in the video *Foundation Subjects MFL: Optional training video*. So, for example, imagine the word to be learned is *quatorze* (the number '14' in French), which pupils often confuse with *quatre* (4). We could model 'word association' by saying 'How am I going to remember this word? What does it sound like in English? catoars … catoars. I know, I'll think of a cat using oars to row a boat'. Encouraging them to draw a picture or do a mime to accompany their 'tip' is particularly helpful for visual and kinaesthetic learners.

Pupils need to experiment with some of the new strategies in the next couple of homeworks and they could comment in the columns in Mim's checklist on p16 on which strategies they tried and whether they were helpful.

Step 3: Action planning

The next step in the cycle of strategy instruction aims to enable pupils to identify their own particular problems and to develop their individual learning plan. It is part and parcel of them developing the learner self-management, referred to in the introduction, but they may need some help in this. As teachers, we may know that if the problem is remembering how to pronounce the words properly, writing them out over and over again is unlikely to improve the situation. Pupils, however, do not always make the link between their particular difficulty and the strategy that is likely to help them overcome it. So it can be useful to encourage them to fill in the 'Memorisation action plan' below which supports them by giving clear guidelines. You may want to ask pupils later to give examples of how they used the strategies they targeted in the third column.

Memorisation action plan

I find it difficult to remember ...	Try ...	Example
the meaning	• thinking of a similar word in English • making pairs with words of opposite meanings • grouping words according to the topic	*Clés* sounds like funny keys made of clay
the pronunciation	• putting the words to a tune • repeating words over and over • recording them on a tape and listening to it	
the spelling	• writing the words out several times • writing the word out backwards • making the word into a picture	
the gender	• underlining words in different colours according to gender • looking for explanations, exceptions; for example, many French words that end in 'e' are feminine but *incendie* is masculine	
Evaluation	• I will do better in vocabulary tests in French • I will do better in my English spelling tests • My learning homework will be quicker/easier/more interesting • I won't be so stuck for words when I am writing • I won't be so stuck for words when I am speaking • I will be more easily understood when I am speaking	

© CILT, the National Centre for Languages 2004

Classic Pathfinder 4: *Doing it for themselves*

The final 'Evaluation' section in the action plan is designed to encourage pupils to share with you the responsibility for measuring their progress and plays a critical role in developing their metacognitive strategies. The focus on understanding the criteria for what counts as 'progress' and measuring themselves against these is evident in the Key Stage 3 'Assessment for Learning' strand. Again, however, initially pupils may need guidelines as to what constitutes progress. The suggestions in the Evaluation section may also encourage pupils to transfer their memorisation strategies from MFL to learning unfamiliar words in English or other subject areas.

The action plan should be stuck into their books with a blank page opposite it for later comments (see Step 5: Evaluation).

Step 4: Extensive practice and Fading out the reminders

In all learning, it is not enough to be told to do something and be shown how. Learning to drive a car or to swim is not simply a matter of following instructions carefully. So, when we teach any topic, we devise a wide range of activities to practise the new language. Strategy instruction is no different and pupils will need a great deal of practice before they can automatically know which strategies to use for any task or vocabulary item they face. Working in pairs or groups has a number of advantages over teacher-centred practice.

Within English teaching, Harrison (2002) argues that collaborative pair and group work is a valuable scaffolding step in shifting from the teacher as 'expert' during the 'modelling' phase to the point at which learners are able to use the strategies independently. The importance of a social community, in which meanings are constructed together and approaches shared, is also underlined in foreign language learning studies by Donato and McCormick (1994) and Lehtonen (2000). Here are some reasons why it is particularly helpful in strategy instruction:

- pupils may be more convinced by each other's positive opinion of the value of a certain strategy than the teacher's exhortations to use it;
- pupils have to reflect on and make explicit the strategies they are using. The language they use to do this and the examples they give may often be more accessible than the teacher's attempt to describe a strategy;
- pupils can learn from each other's learning styles. In Grenfell and Harris (1999) we describe two secondary school pupils. Nick works quickly and confidently, he goes for the overall meaning of the story ('top-down' processing), but pays inadequate attention to detail, failing to confirm any initial guess about what the text is about by double checking it against other clues. Gary is less confident; he uses word-for-word translation, often giving up when he cannot understand the first few words of the text. If these two pupils were invited to work together, 'thinking aloud' what was going on in their heads, they both could benefit by using strategies in combination rather than isolation. 'Borrowing the consciousness of their peers' (Little 1997) is a vital element of strategy instruction; pupils begin to take more responsibility for their own progress and to be less reliant on constant support from the teacher.

What opportunities are there for such pair and group work? In pairs or groups, pupils can:

- brainstorm what strategies they are already using;
- model for each other 'their' preferred strategies;
- try out a new strategy presented by the teacher to learn ten new words;
- try out their partner's strategy to learn new words;
- use 'think aloud' to explain how they are tackling a reading or writing task;
- read a text, each one concentrating on a particular strategy, then share views.

Two words of warning! First, it is important to withdraw these focused 'practice' opportunities gradually; otherwise pupils will simply forget to use their strategies.

Second, it goes without saying that not all pupils know how to work sensibly together. Like all the other strategies, collaborative strategies need to be taught using the steps in the cycle of strategy instruction. You will find an example at the end of this chapter.

Step 5: Evaluation

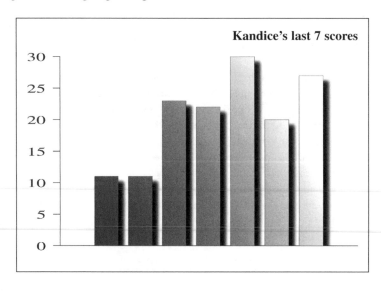

Using new strategies is time-consuming. Pupils tend to prefer the easy, mechanical strategies like copying words down several times. In persuading pupils to persist with the new more demanding strategies, it is helpful for them to have immediate positive feedback. For example, Pamela Dewey produced bar charts plotting their results over a number of vocabulary tests. This also helped her to establish who had fully assimilated the new strategies and who needed more practice.

On the basis of the feedback, pupils can return to their action plan to see if the anticipated progress has or has not been made. If it has, they can move on to trying out some further strategies. For example, if they have assimilated strategies for spelling and meaning, they can target those for gender or pronunciation. However, if there is little improvement, then they need to pinpoint what is going wrong.

Kandice's last 7 scores

This final step does not have to be teacher-centred. In pairs, pupils can discuss the strategies they identified in their action plan and what they will concentrate on now. For homework, they could even write a brief 'diary' entry opposite their 'action plan' on the lines of:

- How did I feel about the new strategies?
- Did they work? Which ones?
- How do I find memorising vocabulary now? Quicker? Easier? More fun?
- What strategies should I try next?

Can plenaries help us with this final step?

Many teachers are currently exploring the role of plenaries in their lessons. They often use them to check what language pupils have learned from the lesson or if they can imagine other situations where they could use it. However, potentially, it is an opportunity to focus not just on the product of the learning but also on the process.

- How did the pupils tackle learning that new language/structure?
- What did they find difficult?
- How did they overcome those difficulties?
- Did their solutions work?
- What can the teacher do to help them with those areas next lesson?
- What can they themselves do to help themselves?

These kinds of discussion may take place at the end of the lesson, but they might also be appropriate mid-way through it, when the issues are still fresh in their minds.

STRATEGIES FOR MEMORISING GRAMMAR RULES

We have seen the cycle of strategy instruction steps illustrated in relation to memorising vocabulary. A similar sequence of steps can be used to teach pupils the strategies for memorising grammar rules. Grammar is currently the source of considerable debate. There seems to be a growing consensus, however, that at some point, once pupils have been exposed to the new structure within a communicative context and have practised it, they should be asked to deduce the rules and encouraged to learn them. Heather Rendall's Pathfinder 33: *Stimulating grammatical awareness* (1998) has a wealth of ideas for teaching grammar. The stage we are focusing on here is how pupils can go about the often tedious process of learning rules. You may want to match the strategies in the list below to the learning styles (visual, auditory, kinaesthetic) that fit them best.

Memorisation strategy	Example
I put rules to music	Singing rules to a tune or a rap, e.g. '*Je suis, tu es, il est*' to the tune of 'Happy birthday'
I make games	Sorting words into piles, e.g. verbs that go with *être* and those that go with *avoir*
I make up a word using the initial letters (acronyms)	E.g. DRAPERS VAN MMT for verbs using *être* and *avoir* in the past tense
I think of a physical response	Thinking of cold/hot for masculine/feminine
I use pictures	Drawing to remember *à la disco/patinoire/piscine* …
I make a linking map	E.g. a topic web for shopping
I use similarities and differences in my mother tongue	E.g. I have hairs brown and eyes blue
I am always on the look out	Underlining all the examples of a rule in a text

Adapted from Oxford (1990)

Before reading on, you might want to think about how you would teach the strategies using the five steps of the instruction cycle described earlier. Some ideas for how to integrate the cycle into the scheme of work are provided in Chapter 4 in relation to listening strategies.

COLLABORATIVE STRATEGIES

This chapter ends with another example of the strategy instruction cycle; this time in relation to the collaborative strategies that were discussed earlier (p19). We include it here as it provides a link to the next chapter on reading and writing strategies, where again pair and group work play a key role. The cross-curricular importance of developing social skills means that the activities suggested below could be carried out either in an MFL lesson or form the focus for a sequence of PSHE lessons.

© CILT, the National Centre for Languages 2004

Awareness -raising	Set up a group work task. After 15 minutes, stop the pupils and ask them how they are going about working together. Brainstorm the strategies they are already using.
Modelling	Ask pupils to think about what makes them comfortable or uneasy when they are in groups in everyday social situations outside school. Discuss also what strategies are needed in the work environment, stressing that, even if they do not particularly like each other, adults need to be able to work together effectively! Ask them to consider the effects of noisy group work on others in the classroom, etc.
Action planning	Pupils draw up a list of 'ground rules' for working together. Pupils' 'ground rules' below (from Harris 1992) shows a list produced by a Year 9 class in a London inner-city school. The list is signed by each group member and displayed on the walls of the classroom. The teacher may want to add some of his or her own ground rules, e.g. 'Ask three other people/look up in a dictionary before you ask the teacher'.
Practice	When groups are not functioning effectively, the teacher reminds them of the ground rules. Reports can provide useful feedback to both pupil and parents as to social skills. It is helpful if pupils frequently change groups, with the aim of ensuring that over the course of the year they have worked with everyone in their class. A good starting point is to tell them that they may work with one friend but they should work with two other people they have not worked with before.
Evaluation	Learners are asked to assess their ability to collaborate and possibly even to comment on their peers' social skills.

© CILT, the National Centre for Languages 2004

**Pupils'
'ground rules'**

Our own rules

e.g.:

1. no bossing
2. give everyone their chance to speak
3. Help each other.
4. Work hard.
5. Don't mess around and distract other people.
6. Give people a chance to express their ideas.
7. Work quietly.
8. Aim for complete work.
9. Wait for others to finish.
10. Be in the lesson as much as possible.

3 The strategy instruction cycle in action: Reading and writing strategies

READING STRATEGIES

Fiona Lunskey, an experienced teacher working in a London comprehensive school, wanted her Year 7 pupils to start to read for pleasure, but she was aware that many of them lacked the basic tools to cope on their own and wanted to explore how to help them. She selected the strategies she wanted to teach from the list opposite, based on those most likely to be within the grasp of the particular age range. Identifying cognates is relatively straightforward, for example, but strategies involving knowledge of the grammar of the language to work out the meaning may be more complex.

Here are some ways of teaching the reading strategies:

Step 1: Awareness raising

Without mentioning strategies, Fiona gave her pupils a text to read for homework 'cold'. Next lesson she asked them what they had done when they 'got stuck' and the class brainstormed the strategies they were already using when they embarked on a text.

Step 2: Modelling

She went on to model the new strategies using the Dutch poem presented at the beginning of this book by thinking aloud, for example; '*appel* sounds like apple in English and *rood* sounds like red. So it could be an apple is red. *Zon* could be sun and that's what's in the little picture, but what does *gelb* mean? Perhaps it means yellow? I'll go on reading and see if the rest of the poem is about colours'.

> E en appel is rood,
> de zon is geel,
> de hemel is blauw,
> een blad is groen,
> een wolk is wit ...
> en de aarde is bruin.

Before reading	✓
I check that I understand the task I have to do	
I look carefully at the title and any pictures to see if I can guess what it will be about	
I try to remember as many words as I can to do with this topic ('brainstorming')	

While reading	✓
I read the whole text through, trying to get an idea of what it is about and ignoring unfamiliar words	
I don't panic when there is something I don't understand, but I carry on reading	
I use my common sense to make sensible guesses	
I pick out cognates and words that look familiar	
I say unfamiliar words out loud, since a word may not look like a cognate, but it may sound like one	
I pick out what I think are the key words	
I look out for the names of people or places	
I use the punctuation for clues, e.g. question marks, capital letters, etc	
I read bits of the text I find hard to understand out loud and try to identify how the sentence breaks down	
I substitute words in English for those I do not know, e.g. 'he *somethinged* his head on the table'	
I break down unfamiliar words and try to associate parts of them with familiar words	
I decide which words I will look up in a dictionary	
I try to spot word categories, e.g. what is a verb, a noun, an adjective	
I pay attention to grammatical clues like tenses or pronouns	

After reading	✓
I check back to see if my first guesses were right and made sense or I need to think again	
I think about why some of the strategies I used did not work and which ones could help me more next time	

© CILT, the National Centre for Languages 2004

Having been exposed to the new strategies, over subsequent lessons pupils engaged in a series of reading tasks so that they could practise the new strategies. The initial task made the use of strategies very explicit:

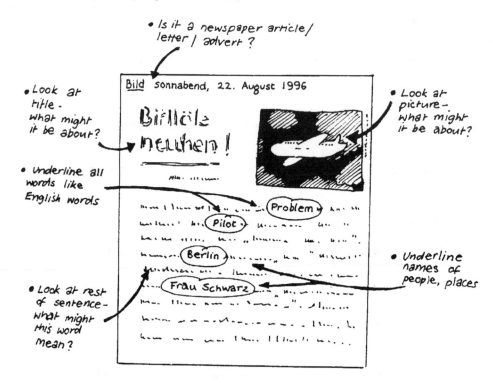

In the next reading task, pupils were reminded of the strategies by filling in the chart, adapted from Ann Swarbrick's *Reading for pleasure in a foreign language* (1990).

German	Looks like English	Guessed	Used word list	Carried on reading	Picture helped	Asked another student	Used dictionary	English
Teufelstich		✓						Boat
Birgit		✓						Bright
machen		✓						Match
Strandbad		✓						Sand

It is interesting to note that the pupil here only used the one strategy of 'guessing' and consistently guessed incorrectly. He appears to use what I call 'wild-card guessing', in other words writing down the first thing that comes into his head! It might be that if he were encouraged to try out some of the other strategies on the list, or if he had worked in a pair with another pupil, his guesses would become more accurate. This is where an action plan can be helpful in helping pupils to identify their own learning approaches and how to tackle the difficulties they cause.

Step 3: Action planning

My difficulty	Try ...
I panic as soon as I see all those words that I do not understand	*looking first for the words you do know and for the cognates*
I try to translate each word and then give up because I have to look up everything in the dictionary	*reading the whole passage through first. Use your common sense, the pictures and title to get a general idea of what it might be about*
I read the whole passage and make a guess about what it is about, but often I am wrong	*reading it again. Look up key words that you do not know in the dictionary. Then be prepared to change your mind about what it is about*
Evaluation	• *I will find reading quicker/easier/more interesting* • *I won't need to use a dictionary so much* • *I will be able to read longer texts like magazine articles or from the Internet*

Step 4: Practice

Two student teachers, Natalie Mendes and Augusta Viera decided to practise the strategies within a group work situation so that their Year 9 pupils could share the way they used their new strategies and to give them more confidence in reading independently. Twelve short texts from popular magazines were chosen, colour copied and laminated. The class was divided into groups of four and each group had to complete at least two texts. Before the group as a whole shared their ideas on what the text meant, each individual member chose one strategy from their action plan on which to focus and indicated on a sheet what 'their' strategy had helped them to understand, giving examples. In the event, the pupils' comments showed that they were not certain what was required. So, for the following lesson, the teachers decided to structure the group work more tightly, giving pupils the following directions:

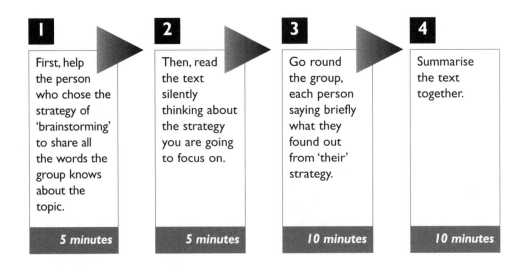

1	2	3	4
First, help the person who chose the strategy of 'brainstorming' to share all the words the group knows about the topic.	Then, read the text silently thinking about the strategy you are going to focus on.	Go round the group, each person saying briefly what they found out from 'their' strategy.	Summarise the text together.
5 minutes	**5 minutes**	**10 minutes**	**10 minutes**

Step 5: Evaluation

After further practice, both in class and for homework, pupils return to their action plan, so that they learn to evaluate their progress for themselves and to set themselves new targets. For some pupils, this might mean paying greater attention to grammatical clues. For others, it might mean 'double checking' that their first guesses were correct.

WRITING STRATEGIES AND STRATEGIES FOR CHECKING WRITTEN WORK

Katrin Artz, a student teacher working in a boys' comprehensive school in East London, wanted to stretch her top set Year 7 to produce more extended writing.

Step 1: Awareness-raising

As they were a new class, she set them for homework the task of writing her a letter to tell them a bit about themselves. The next lesson, she brainstormed with them how they had gone about their writing and produced the checklist opposite.

Step 2: Modelling

The next topic in the scheme of work was 'My ideal holiday' and Katrin introduced some of the basic vocabulary. Then, in order to model some of the strategies under 'preparing to write', she asked pupils to put the title 'Holidays' in the centre of a brainstorming spidergram and to work in pairs to write down around it any key ideas that came to mind. If they could remember the words, they wrote them in German on the left-hand side of the spidergram. If they could not remember them, they wrote them in English on the right-hand side. She also encouraged them to think of which

<u>Writing in German – that is easy!!!</u>
<u>Tick the strategies you use!</u>

	Preparing to write		
1	Developing Ideas I think about what the task requires and brainstorm some ideas of what I want to say; in English if I am a beginner and in German if I can		✓
2	Gathering familiar language I try to remember relevant words or phrases that I have previously learned to do with this topic		✓
3	I remind myself of other familiar language by looking at my coursebook and my exercise book		
4	I list good phrases and expressions that I could use		✓
5	Organising ideas I decide how to organise my ideas by writing a rough plan to show the order in which I will put them		✓
	while writing		
6	a friend and I write it together, sitting together at a computer		
7	I put 2 or 3 chunks of language that I know together to make a new sentence		
8	I add ideas as I write		
9	As I write, I re-read each sentence and translate it back into English to check if it makes sense		✓
	Making it fancy – extending the language		
10	I try to include as much detail as possible (for example when I'm describing something or someone)		✓
11	I try to use 'linking' words (und, oder, aber)		✓
	After writing		
12	I use the strategies for checking my written work		✓
13	I check the punctuation and the spelling		✓

words can go together like adjectives with the nouns (big, expensive, nice) and to use 'chunks of language' they already knew from 'Hobbies' and other topics they had previously covered.

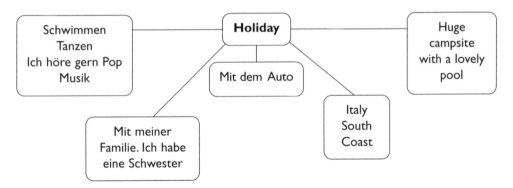

She then told them to organise their ideas in the sequence in which they would present them in a written account. For example, would they start by saying where they went and how they got there, then where they stayed, etc? She then modelled some of the other strategies on her checklist. (See Macaro 2001 for some very useful ideas for teaching writing strategies.)

Step 3: Action planning

Once pupils have experimented with some of the new strategies, they are ready to identify their own personal needs and targets. In drawing up an action plan, the following guidance can be useful:

My difficulty	Try ...
My mind goes blank and I don't have any ideas	*thinking about what you would say in English*
My mind goes blank and I can't think of any words I know	• *looking back in your book and in your coursebook.* • *using spidergrams*
I get very muddled about what to put first	*listing all your main ideas and then trying to put them in order*
It seems to me that I write like a five year-old baby	*to find sample texts and copy expressions used*

Evaluation	
	• *What I write will be longer* • *What I write will be more interesting for me to write and for others to read!* • *I will express what I think better*

Step 4: Practice

Clearly it will take pupils a lot of time to assimilate these new strategies and they will need constant reminders and frequent opportunities to work in pairs or groups on joint writing tasks.

Step 5: Evaluation

Pupils can also work together in the evaluation process. The CILT publication, *Effective assessment in MFL* (Barnes and Hunt 2003: 102), includes a chart which is designed to help pupils evaluate their own and each other's oral presentations. It could easily be adapted so that they give each other feedback on a written text.

STRATEGIES FOR CHECKING WRITTEN WORK

Under 'After writing' (p31), Katrin Artz has listed several strategies for checking work. It is worth perhaps expanding on them as they are skills that apply across the curriculum and are more complex than we initially think. We often respond to the cry 'I've finished, Miss' with 'Well, read it over again and correct any mistakes'. The completed work is handed in, but it is not unusual to encounter frequent mistakes in gender, tense and word order. I have to confess to feeling immensely frustrated when my own children asked me to help them with their homework. I would remind them to check it first before they showed it to me. After five minutes, they would return, assuring me they had checked everything, but as soon as I pointed to a particular word, they would comment with surprise, 'Oh, yes, it needs another e'! Frustrating though this is, it is perhaps understandable why pupils find checking their work so difficult, if we reflect on the processes involved that we as successful linguists use to check our work.

After writing	
I read the text all the way through to see if it makes sense	
I read each word separately to see if the spelling 'looks right'	
I say each sentence to myself to see if it 'sounds right'	
I read the text over again, paying attention to the grammatical mistakes I usually make, e.g.: • adjectival agreement • verb endings • tenses	
I make sure that the style is appropriate and I use good 'linking' words (connectives)	
I try to spot what I am still not sure of	
I look it up	
I leave it for a day and then come back to read it 'with fresh eyes'	
I give it to a friend to read	

It is probable that many of our pupils are not aware that we mean them to do all these things when we tell them to check their work, and that if they use the strategies they will be able to spot more of their mistakes for themselves. How then do we go about teaching them?

Step 1: Awareness-raising

In line with the cycle of strategy instruction, we could set them a written homework and remind them to check it carefully, without going into any detail about **how** to check it.

Step 2: Modelling

This could lead into a discussion about what pupils did when they checked their work and we can model any unfamiliar strategies not already described by members of the class. To demonstrate how to check for meaning, for example, Lindsey Hand, when a student teacher, asked them to spot the mistakes in a simple text:

> Ich heiße Kerstin. Ich wohne in Berlin in einem Zweifamilienhaus. Ich bin Einzelkind, aber ich habe einen Hund und eine Katze. Ich bin sehr sportlich. Ich spiele nicht gern Fußball und Tennis. Sport ist langweilig. Ich habe zwei Brüder.

Although there is always a danger in presenting pupils with the wrong spellings, for the purpose of modelling 'checking if it looks right', she then asked them to ring the correct word:

Schwimbad   *Schwimmbad*
geradaus   *geradeaus*

In French, similar mistakes often occur with:

campagne   *campange*
mansion   *maison*

In terms of 'checking if it sounds right', pupils first need some initial exposure to the language and some understanding of the rules. For example, verbs that go with *avoir* and *être* in the past tense could be introduced in the context of a pop star's recent world tour. Pupils' ears can then be 'tuned in' to noticing the differences by the teacher reading out ten sentences either with an *avoir* or an *être* verb in them. Pupils tick in the appropriate column of the grid below:

	avoir	*être*
1		
2		
3		

Then, the teacher could read out another ten sentences, some of which are correct and some incorrect. Pupils should be encouraged to check 'if they sound right' before placing a tick or a cross.

Step 3: Action planning

Having modelled the strategies with her pupils, and given them a checklist, Pam Harkness, a student teacher, discovered a useful (and less time-consuming way) of giving feedback on pupils' written work. As you can see on p33, she wrote several of the most significant mistakes at the bottom of the page and next to each the number of the strategy that would help them avoid it. Strategy 12 in her checklist was 'I check the little bits – accents and endings'. Strategy 13 was 'I check my tenses with my verb Help Sheet and/or my book'.

Pam's feedback was a good preparation for filling in their action plan.

J'ai mange le plats typique pour ma petite dejeuner. En le
l'appres midi nous avons le promenade.
Le Mardi J'ai danser dans la desôtel et en le Matin J'ai
nage dans la piscine.
Le Mecredi Je me suis reposée et je me suis restée
dans ma chambre dans l'hôtel. Oh oui... J'ai joue au tennis
et J'ai nage dans la piscine encour une fois!
Le Vendredi Je suis allee une restaurant Grec avec
ma mere, le service etait affreux parce que nous attendu et
attendu et ma diner etait froud ma mere regarder une arrai-
ner nager dans le soupe.
Le Samedi et J'ai une fievre et J'ai etait vomir,
J'ai pense que etait le diner en le vendredi vrai, Parce que
J'ai etait misérables parce que J'ai de la fievre ma mere
visite le monument types historique car et fait de la promenade.

* le musique etait tres rapide

```
What's missing?                    Level 6+

J'ai mange (1)  Str 12.
Je suis allee (2)
                        ⊕  See
What's wrong?              Helpsheet
J'ai danser   Str. 13
  (No 1)
```

17

My difficulty	Try ...
I cannot bring myself to re-read/check what I have written	*leaving it for a day and then coming back to it*
I make silly spelling mistakes	*writing down two possible spellings and seeing which 'looks right'*
I keep making the same grammar mistakes	• *checking the little bits — accents and endings* • *making up a list of your 'favourite' mistakes and sticking it in the back of your book. Then cross them out as they become less frequent*
Evaluation	• *I won't make so many mistakes in my French* • *I won't make so many mistakes in my other written work* • *I won't feel so frustrated when I get my work back* • *I will feel more confident about trying out new expressions and grammar rules* • *I will know what to look up in the dictionary or grammar book*

Step 4: Practice

To remind pupils to use 'their' strategies, we could ask them to fill in the table 'Checking my written work' opposite each time they hand in any further written work. Item 4 could be altered according to the particular grammar point focused on. Insisting that pupils record at least one point that they looked up should develop the habit of using the dictionary and other reference books. Asking them at the end to identify what it is that they feel may still be wrong, inspite of the careful checking, serves a number of purposes. While the onus for 'getting it right' has been placed so far on the pupil, it is also important to acknowledge a legitimate role for the teacher, in which pupil and teacher can work together to overcome specific problems and a dialogue can be entered into, albeit it in a written form. The pupil's comments may also provide the teacher with some insight into areas of confusion that are either specific to that learner or may be shared by other members of the class.

Put a star * by the special strategies you chose for your action plan.

Strategy	One mistake I corrected
1. Does it make sense?	
2. Does it sound right?	
3. Does it look right?	
4. Checking for my most usual mistakes: • • •	
5. Is the style right?	
6. Word looked up	
7. What I am still unsure of. I know it's wrong but I am not sure why or how to find out about it	
Teacher's feedback	

Step 5: Evaluation

In an ideal world, it would be good to encourage pupils to reflect at this point not only on their MFL written work but also on their work in other subject areas. Hopefully the KS3 Strategy will encourage cross-curricular transfer both in terms of the pupils' perceptions and also teachers' awareness of how they can complement each other's initiatives. Within MFL, and depending on their attainment level, pupils can be encouraged to focus on strategies to promote greater accuracy or a more elaborate style, or both.

We have seen in this chapter that the aim is not only to put the responsibility onto pupils for their own learning, but to provide them with a clear framework for how to go about it.

The question that inevitably arises is how to fit this kind of systematic teaching of the different strategies into an already overcrowded timetable. We discuss this issue in the next chapter, along with the use of the target language.

4   Issues in strategy instruction

This chapter discusses some of the important questions raised by teachers during INSET sessions and tries to offer some solutions.

 ## WHAT TO TEACH WHEN?

First, it may be easier both for teacher and pupils to focus on one skill area at a time. Second, it is worth taking at least a term to complete the cycle of strategy instruction with that skill area. That way you can provide enough practice for the strategies to be fully assimilated, although of course pupils may still need reminders to use them.

In choosing which strategies to teach within that skill area, it is worth considering:

- which are the easier and which are more complex; in reading, for example, clues that are dependent on grammatical knowledge are probably more complex than cognates;
- which are the easier to teach and which are more difficult.

So it is not as easy and straightforward as saying 'teach memorisation strategies to Year 7, teach reading strategies to Year 8, etc'. We can, however, talk about different levels of complexity of strategy. You start at a fairly simple level and when your pupils have some command of that strategy, you introduce the next level. We probably need to tackle it as a spiral, teaching perhaps basic reading strategies early on, but then introducing more complex ones when pupils are ready for it. This does involve some serious planning to ensure progression over Key Stages 3 and 4.

The table 'Guidelines for what to teach when' (from Harris et al 2001a: 145) opposite provides suggestions in terms of which strategies seem, from our experiences at least, to be the easiest to teach. While not based on any empirical research, we believe it would be foolish to ignore teachers' intuitive reactions.

From easy to hard steps	Skill area	Possible reasons
1	Memorisation	These are very much conscious actions that we do to learn words and therefore it is easier for pupils to explain what they already do and for teachers to model new strategies.
2	Reading	Although some of what successful readers do is at an unconscious level, at least with reading (unlike listening), there is time to go back to a hard word or phrase and reflect on the best strategies to try, etc. So teachers can work through the text one step at a time, modelling how to tackle it.
3	Listening	This is more fleeting than reading, but as a receptive skill is more under control than spontaneous speech. An example of how to teach listening strategies is given below.
4	Checking written work	Much of what we do here is dependent on a certain level of grammatical knowledge.
5	Speaking strategies	These are hard to **use**. Faced with someone who expects an immediate response, we don't have time when we are 'stuck' to think 'now what strategy would help me best?'! Speaking strategies are also hard to **teach**, since they are in part dependent on teachers providing listening materials which model what the learners should be doing. A checklist of speaking strategies is provided in the next chapter.

 ## THERE'S NO TIME! BUILDING THE CYCLE INTO THE SCHEME OF WORK

Listening strategies

At first sight, strategy instruction looks extremely time-consuming and there may be concerns about how to make the space to include it in the scheme of work. It is worth exploring just how much extra time may be involved, by taking a practical example of integrating the teaching of listening strategies into the scheme of work in the context of the topic 'Hobbies'. First, here is a list of listening strategies that successful linguists use:

Checklist of listening strategies

Before listening	✓
I check that I understand the task I have to do	
I look carefully at the title and any pictures to see if I can guess what it will be about	
I try to remember as many words as I can to do with this topic	
I think about what is likely to be said in this situation and predict the words I am likely to hear	

While listening	✓
I work out if it is a conversation, an advert, a news bulletin, etc	
I pay attention to the tone of voice and any background noises for clues	
I use other clues like key words to identify the rough gist	
I use my common sense to make sensible guesses	
I try to see if any words are like words in English	
I don't panic when there is something I don't understand, but I carry on listening	
I listen out for the names of people or places	
I try to hold the difficult sounds in my head and say them over and over again	
I try to break down the stream of sounds into individual words and write them down to see if they are like words I recognise	
I don't give up and just make wild guesses	
I listen out for grammar clues like tenses, pronouns	

After listening	✓
I check back to see if my first guesses were right and made sense or I need to think again	
I think about why some of the strategies I used did not work and which could help me more next time	

Clearly, teaching methods will differ and the suggestions overleaf in 'Integrating listening strategies into the scheme of work' only provide the 'bare bones' of the cycle of strategy instruction in relation to listening activities. There will, of course, be the usual speaking, reading and writing activities going on in each lesson. Nevertheless, they hopefully show how the cycle can be part and parcel of everyday lessons and need not take too much extra time. At an INSET session, the teachers and I worked out that the extra time involved would be 70 minutes over 10 lessons (the 'extra' time is indicated in italics in the first column). As the teachers pointed out, in the end your pupils actually **gain time**. Instead of only being able to understand every listening text if you patiently work through it with them, they have a multitude of strategies enabling them to tackle new texts on their own.

What about the target language?

How much of the strategy instruction can be given in the target language? The checklists can be written in the target language, provided they are accompanied by visual support. Perhaps even the action plan could be in the target language, if pupils were given a list of possible expressions from which to choose. With most pre-sixth-form classes, however, it is likely that the discussions in Lessons 3, 5 and 10 of the 'Listening' scheme of work (see pp40–41) would have to be in English initially. The aim here is to get all pupils participating and reflecting on their learning. The effort of explaining themselves in the target language may well deter all but the highest attainers from contributing to the discussion. Similarly, the pair work may well take place in English, as pupils explain to each other how they are tackling a text or checking their written work. In the long term, any disadvantages produced by not using the target language one hundred per cent of the time may be offset by an improvement in pupil performance, independence and motivation. As the *KS3 MFL Framework* notes (p26), 'teachers may need to use some English judiciously for carefully specified purposes in some parts of a lesson'.

As pupils begin to become familiar with the process of reflecting on their own learning, however, we can scaffold a gradual shift to using the target language by displaying key expressions around the classroom. Explaining that *'je trouve ça difficile'* applies equally well to difficulties encountered in memorising vocabulary, as it does to different school subjects, with the added bonus that how they approach their language learning may well be of more immediate concern than whether they do or do not like Geography, Maths, etc. As Little (1993) points out:

> The learner's acceptance of responsibility for his or her learning entails the
> gradual development of a capacity for independent and flexible use of the
> target language. Thus, all autonomy projects will necessarily tend to create the
> circumstances in which learners are engaged in activities that require them to
> use the target language for genuinely communicative purposes.

Issues such as time and target language cannot be resolved easily. Answers will vary according to the class taught, to the school situation and departmental priorities. They can, however, be discussed in departmental meetings and in the last chapter, you will find some suggestions for exploring strategy instruction within your own school context.

Integrating listening strategies into the scheme of work

Lesson	Activities	Stage of cycle
1 and 2	Teach/revise vocabulary and structures of the topic 'hobbies' (present tense).	
3	Don't tell pupils the lesson will be about strategies. Give them a listening task to do 'cold', e.g. play a tape where various speakers identify their favourite hobbies. Check answers.	Awareness raising
(20 mins)	Ask pupils what they did when they did not understand words or phrases in the tape.	
	Brainstorm a list of listening strategies.	
	Model strategies such as 'identify the text or topic', 'predict likely words', 'make sensible guesses', etc.	Modelling of some new strategies
4	Teach/revise vocabulary and structures of the topic 'hobbies' (past tense).	
	Play a tape. Each group of pupils focuses on one specific strategy and feeds back what they have understood to the rest of the class.	
(20 mins)	Teacher models the strategy of 'using grammatical clues' (past and present tenses). For each sentence the teacher reads out, pupils tick under the correct column: **Present tense**　　　**Past tense** 1 2 3 Finally, in pairs, pupils are given a transcript of the tape and identify what other strategies they could have used to help them overcome any difficulties.	Modelling of other new strategies

Integrating listening strategies into the scheme of work

Lesson	Activities	Stage of cycle
5 (5 mins) (15 mins)	Give pupils a typed-up checklist of the listening strategies identified in lessons 3 and 4. Play a more complex tape. Pupils in pairs compare their answers and how they arrived at them. Teacher plays tape again and checks answers. He or she prepares them for the action-planning stage by asking them about their learning style. Do they tend to try to translate every word and then panic or do they make a rough guess at the overall meaning and then fail to check back carefully to make sure their initial guess was correct? Homework: to fill in action plan	Action planning
6	Teacher teaches more new vocabulary and structures. He or she plays tape and asks pupils to apply the strategies they identified on their action plan.	Practice
7	Teacher returns action plans with comments. During individual or group work on the new topic (e.g. reading/writing activities) he or she discusses action plans with those individual pupils who chose inappropriate strategies.	
8/9	New topic, includes tapes where pupils are reminded to use the strategies they identified on their action plans. Ideally, there are opportunities for pupils to listen to tapes in groups or take cassettes home to listen to for homework, so that they can play back over and over again the sections they personally found hard. The 'Independendent listening worksheet' overleaf could guide them in their use of strategies	
10 (10 mins)	New topic. Discussion: how are pupils now finding listening to tapes? Have their marks improved? What strategies do they now need to concentrate on? For example, if they tended to panic if they did not understand each word and are now more able to listen for the whole gist, are they ready to listen out for grammatical clues?	Evaluation and further action planning

Independent listening worksheet

1 Type of text? Conversation/news report/train announcement …

2 Topic? Records/arrangements to meet/family problems

3 Predict and compare

What English words are likely in this situation?	Do we know the French word for them?	Tick if heard	Other words we recognised

4 Play the recording again. Use your common sense: is there anything else you can guess now?

5 Problems? Play it again: what do you still not understand? Say the sounds over and over; try to write them down.

6 Can you guess anything more from clues from the ends of words or the word order?

7 Look at the transcript. Underline the sections you didn't understand. Can you work out what they mean now? Are there any strategies that could have helped you work them out earlier?

I could have used the strategy of _____ to guess _____

_____

5 Strategy instruction in each school context

Every school is different, every class is different and we as teachers are all different. If we want pupils to reflect on their own learning and to take greater responsibility for making progress, what are the implications for us as their teachers? Could we also undertake a similar process of reflection but in relation to our teaching?

It is interesting to note that the cycle of strategy instruction is very similar to the cycle of action-based research, which helps teachers to evaluate systematically new initiatives they try out with their classes. Given all the new challenges teachers are faced with, having a sense of being able to make a personal, well-informed, professional judgement about what 'works' and doesn't work' seems particularly important.

Step 1: What's the problem?

Just as the pupils start the cycle by taking stock of what they are already doing, we may begin by identifying the problems of a particular class and how we currently approach teaching them. What is the immediate area of concern with these pupils and which strategies could be taught to address it? It might be the need to encourage more extensive reading with Year 8 or to ensure that Year 11 pupils check their work more carefully.

Step 2: What would help?

Identify which skill area and which strategies would be relevant for addressing the problem. There is little point in teaching strategies that pupils are already using. Although it may be helpful to use the checklists as a starting point, it may be necessary to add to them by:

- observing which strategies high attainers in the class are already using to tackle that skill area successfully;
- observing which strategies appear to be lacking among the low attainers in the class;
- observing successful strategies used by any older students in Year 11 or the sixth form that could be passed on to the class in question;
- reflecting on our own use of strategies. What was it that helped us to become successful linguists?

Step 3: Cross-curricular liaison

The *KS3 Framework for Teaching English*, the 'Progress Units' and the emphasis in the *Learning challenge* on 'organisation', 'memory' and 'reflection' all mean that it can be very useful to liaise with English, PSHE, and SEN colleagues to find out what strategies pupils are familiar with so that you can make the links.

Step 4: Make it user-friendly

Put the strategies into words that pupils will understand and relate to. Again, liaising with other colleagues may help so you all use the same terminology.

Step 5: Decide which strategies to teach first

Two student teachers, Cheryl Michael and Heather Wright, for example, found that by teaching pupils to recognise cognates first, they gained their trust and their interest and were able to go on to more complex strategies.

Step 6: Planning to teach

Build the cycle into the scheme of work, deciding when to start it, how to integrate it into subsequent lessons, etc.

Step 7: Resourcing

Make any necessary materials: a checklist, poster or other ways of reminding pupils of the strategies. If you can involve other colleagues in the department in trying out strategy instruction with their classes too, the workload can be shared and findings compared.

Step 8: Planning to evaluate

Just as the pupils in their action plans decide how they will measure their progress, it is helpful to establish from the outset how you will know what 'works' and 'doesn't work'. Has the problem diminished, stayed the same or even got worse? Of course, you will gain a lot of information just from seeing how pupils respond in class, the quality of their work and so on. But could tests or questionnaires give you a fuller picture? If you are working with a student teacher, could they be involved, for example by interviewing a small sample of pupils?

Step 9: Evaluating

Did the strategy instruction appear to justify the time taken and the use of English? Is there any long-term improvement in the problem area identified? Have all pupils benefited from the strategy instruction or only a limited number? Who has failed to try out new strategies? Why? What do the pupils think of it themselves?

Step 10: What's the problem?

Often the very process of tackling a problem head-on throws up new issues and so the cycle starts again, both for us and our pupils. It may be that pupils still need more practice. It may be that you decide on ways of 'tightening up' the instruction to involve more pupils or increase the use of the target language.

 ## SPEAKING STRATEGIES

To 'trial run' putting some of these ideas into practice, let's take speaking strategies. These are also known as communication strategies and are generally defined as the strategies we use when our linguistic repertoire is not big enough to allow us to say what we want to say. Perhaps you recognise yourself in the picture Dörnyei (1995: 57) paints?

> *Some people can communicate effectively in an L2 with only 100 words. How do they do it? They use their hands, they imitate the sound or movement of things, they mix languages, they create new words, they describe or circumlocute something they don't know the word for; in short, they use communication strategies.*

As you read through the checklist of speaking strategies overleaf, think about which class needs them most and tick the strategies that you think would be most relevant to them. Clearly, more advanced pupils should aim to apply some of the strategies Katrin Artz indicated for writing (see pp28–30); for example 'making it fancy' and aiming for accuracy are important in speaking as well as writing. We know from research, however (Skehan and Foster 1997), that beginning learners find it difficult to create the 'mental space' needed to produce the language spontaneously, while at the same time making it as detailed and complex as possible and checking for accuracy. So some of the strategies are aimed at pupils who are simply struggling to be able to say anything at all!

Practising speaking	✓
I play with sounds. (Young Pathfinder 5: *First steps to reading and writing* (Skarbek 1998) has a host of phrases put to simple tunes and poems)	
I look at the teacher or at native speakers talking on video and imitate the shape of their mouths	
I listen to the radio/cassettes and repeat out loud useful expressions I hear	
I count /say hard phrases when I walk to school/am sitting on the bus	
As I move through my day, I name what I see around me (e.g. trees, people, cars, furniture, books)	
As I move through my day, I say out loud what I am doing: 'Now I am drinking a cup of coffee/walking to the bus stop/doing my homework'	
I think about what I would like to say and look up any words I don't know in the dictionary	

Before speaking	✓
I think about what I want to say	
I remind myself of how to greet people, to say 'thank you', etc	
I remind myself of words and expressions that I already know and put them into sentences	
I look up words I don't know or ask the teacher or a friend	

Checklist of speaking strategies

While speaking	✓
I try to keep it simple and avoid topics or ideas that may be particularly difficult	
I use familiar phrases that I am confident with to give myself time to think of how to say something I am less sure of	
I use 'hesitation' expressions like 'well', 'you know', etc to give myself time to think	
I listen out for words and expressions that I have just heard the teacher or my partner say and try to use them myself	
And if I do not know the word for something …	
I describe it, e.g. what it looks like, what you can use it for, whether you wear, eat or drink it!	
I use opposites like 'not married' for 'single'	
I use a word that has roughly the same meaning, like 'boat' instead of 'ship'	
I use mime or a gesture or a facial expression	
I make up a word by saying the English word but with the foreign accent	
I use an 'all-purpose' word like 'thingie'	
I ask for help, e.g. 'how do you say …./what do you call …?'	
I show I need help, e.g. by pausing, a puzzled expression, etc	

After speaking	✓
I write down the words or grammar rules that I did not know and look them up	
I think about why some of the strategies I used did not work and what I could do next time	

© CILT, the National Centre for Languages 2004

Speaking strategies are particularly difficult to teach, so before filling in the table 'Planning for strategy instruction' below you may find it useful to look at Chapter 2 of the CILT publication, *Something to say: Promoting spontaneous classroom talk* (Harris, Burch, Jones and Darcy 2001b: 39–42) for ideas on how to teach pupils to paraphrase. Chapter 4 of *Helping learners learn: Exploring strategy instruction in language classrooms across Europe* (Harris et al 2001a) has some activities for teaching 'hesitation strategies' or 'fillers' and examples of how the student teachers used tests, questionnaires and tape recordings to evaluate the outcomes of the strategy instruction they undertook.

Planning for strategy instruction	
What is my most amenable class that I could try this out on?	
Which strategies would be most useful/teachable for them?	
Which strategies are they already doing?	
How will I teach the strategies using the cycle of strategy instruction? • Awareness-raising • Modelling • Action planning • Practice • Evaluation	
What useful resources could I use?	
What worked/didn't work?	
Who shall I try it with next?	

A FINAL THOUGHT

The reality is that experimenting with a new teaching approach can be time-consuming and even daunting, so it is often easiest to iron out any 'teething problems' with a fairly amenable class! But if we are prepared to take the risk of trying out the strategy instruction cycle, it may not only enable the pupils to take greater responsibility for their progress and discover more about how they learn, we may also come to a greater understanding of the learning process ourselves. As Leni Dam (1990), a pioneer in the movement towards greater pupil autonomy, pointed out:

> *The pivot of the whole learning/teaching process is, without doubt, the recurring evaluation, a constant focus for both teacher and learner on: What am I doing? > Why am I doing it? > How am I doing it? > What can it be used for?*

These questions are also of key importance in Part 2 of this book: 'Words: Teaching and learning vocabulary'.

Appendix

Translation of the poem on p8:

An apple is red,
the sun is yellow,
the sky is blue,
a leaf is green,
a cloud is white …
and the earth is brown.

And would you now be able
to answer the question:
What colour is love?

References

Barnes, A. and Hunt, M. (2003) *Effective assessment in MFL*. CILT.

Cohen, A. D. (ed) (1998) *Strategies in learning and using a second language*. Longman.

Council for Cultural Co-operation Education Committee (1996) *Modern Languages: Learning, teaching and assessment. A Common European Framework of Reference*. Strasbourg: Council of Europe.

Dam, L. (1990) 'Learner autonomy in practice' in Gathercole, I. (ed), *Autonomy in language learning*. CILT.

Department for Education and Employment (1998) *The National Literacy Strategy*. HMSO.

Department for Education and Employment (1999) *Modern Foreign Languages in the National Curriculum*. HMSO.

Department for Education and Employment/Qualifications and Curriculum Authority (2000) *Modern Foreign Languages. A scheme of work for Key Stage 3*. HMSO.

Department for Education and Skills (2001a) *Key Stage 3 Literacy Progress Units*. HMSO.

Department for Education and Skills (2001b) *Key Stage 3 National Strategy. Framework for Teaching English: Years 7, 8 and 9*. HMSO.

Department for Education and Skills (2003a) *Key Stage 3 National Strategy. Framework for Teaching Modern Foreign Languages: Years 7, 8 and 9*. HMSO.

Department for Education and Skills (2003b) *The learning challenge*. HMSO.

Department for Education and Skills (2003c) *Teaching and learning in secondary schools: Pilot*. HMSO.

Dickinson, L. (1987) *Self-instruction in language learning*. Cambridge University Press.

Donato, R. and McCormick, D. E. (1994) 'A socio-cultural perspective on language learning strategies: the role of mediation'. *The Modern Language Journal*, 78 (iv): 453–64.

Dörnyei, Z. (1995) 'On the teachability of communication strategies'. *TESOL Quarterly*, 29, 1: 55–80.

Gardner, H. (1993) *The unschooled mind: How children think and how schools should teach.* Harper Collins.

Graham, S. and Rees, F. (1995) 'Gender differences in language learning: the question of control'. *Language Learning Journal,* 11: 18–19.

Grenfell, M. and Harris, V. (1993) 'How do pupils learn? (Part 1)'. *Language Learning Journal,* 8: 22–25.

Grenfell, M. and Harris, V. (1999) *Modern Languages and learning strategies: In theory and practice.* Routledge.

Harris, V. and Grenfell, M. (forthcoming) 'Language learning strategies: A case for cross curricular collaboration'. *Language Awareness.*

Harris, V. (1992) Pathfinder 14: *Fair enough? Equal opportunities and Modern Languages.* CILT.

Harris, V., with Gaspar, A., Jones, B., Ingvarsdottir, H., Palos, I., Neuburg, R. and Schindler, I. (2001a) *Helping learners learn: Exploring strategy instruction in language classrooms across Europe.* Austria: European Centre for Modern Languages.

Harris, V., Burch, J., Jones, B. and Darcy, J. (2001b) *Something to say? Promoting spontaneous classroom talk.* CILT.

Harris, V. (2003) 'Adapting classroom-based strategy instruction to a distance learning context'. *TESL-EJ Special issue: Strategy Research and Training,* 7: 2.1–16.

Harrison, C. (2002) *The Key Stage 3 National Strategy. Key Stage 3 English: Roots and research.* Department for Education and Skills/HMSO.

Holec, H. (ed) (1988) *Autonomy and self-directed learning: Present fields of application* Strasbourg: Council of Europe.

Johnstone, R., Low, L., Duffield, J. and Brown, S. (1993) *Evaluating foreign languages in primary schools.* Scottish CILT.

Jones, B. and Jones, G. (2001) *Boys' performance in Modern Foreign Languages: Listening to learners.* CILT.

Jones, B. and Swarbrick, A. (2004) New Pathfinder 4: *It makes you think! Creating engagement, offering challenges.* CILT.

Lehtonen, T. (2000) 'Awareness of strategies is not enough: How learners can give each other the confidence to use them'. *Language Awareness,* 9 (2): 64–76.

Little, D. (1991) *Learner autonomy 1: Definitions, issues and problems.* Dublin: Authentik.

Little, D. (1993) 'Learning as dialogue: The dependence of learner autonomy on teacher autonomy'. Symposium on Learner Autonomy at AILA 93: Amsterdam.

Little, D. (1997) 'Strategies in language learning and teaching: Some introductory reflections'. Paper given at CILT Research Forum: 'Strategies in foreign language learning'. CILT.

Macaro, E. (2001) *Strategies in foreign and second language classrooms: Learning to learn.* Cassell.

O'Malley, J. M. and Chamot, A. U. (1990) *Learning strategies in second language acquisition.* Cambridge University Press.

Nunan, D. (1995) 'Closing the gap between learning and instruction'. *TESOL Quarterly,* 29: 133–158.

Oxford, R. (1990), *Language learning strategies.* Heinle and Heinle.

Qualifications and Curriculum Authority (1999) *Curriculum 2000: Implementing the changes to 16–19 qualifications.* Qualifications and Curriculum Authority.

Rendall, H. (1998) Pathfinder 33: *Stimulating grammatical awareness: A fresh look at language acquisition.* CILT.

Rubin, J. (1990) 'How learner strategies can inform language teaching'. In: Bickley, V. (ed) *Language use, language teaching and the curriculum.* Hong Kong: Institute of Language in Education.

Rubin, J. (2001) 'Language learner self-management'. *Journal of Asian Pacific Communications* 11 (1): 25–37.

Skarbek, C. (1998) Young Pathfinder 5: *First steps to reading and writing.* CILT.

Skehan, P. and Foster, P. (1997) 'Task type and task processing conditions as influences on foreign language performance'. *Language Teaching Research* 1(3): 185–211.

Swarbrick, A. (1990) Pathfinder 2: *Reading for pleasure in a foreign language.* CILT.

Vygotsky, L. S. (1962) *Thought and language.* Cambridge, MA: MIT Press.

Vygotsky, L.S. (1978) *Mind in society.* Cambridge, MA: Harvard University Press.

Walsh Anglund, J. (1968) *Welke kleur heeft de liefde?.* Holland: Zomer & Keuning.

FURTHER READING

Chamot, A. U., Barnhardt, S., El-Dinary, P. B. and Robbins, J. (1999) *The learning strategies handbook.* New York State: Longman.

McDonough, S. H. (1999) 'Learner strategies: State of the art article'. *Language Teaching,* 32: 1–18.

McDonough, S. H. (1995) *Strategy and skill in learning a foreign language.* Edward Arnold.

Wenden, A. (1991) *Learner strategies for learner autonomy.* Prentice Hall.

Part 2

Words
Teaching and learning
vocabularly

DAVID SNOW

Introduction

words *which are 'taught'* & words *which are 'caught'*

There are basically two ways of 'getting' new vocabulary:

- **conscious learning** of specific words which have been 'taught' by the teacher;
- sub-conscious **absorption** of words as they crop up incidentally.

Several studies into the acquisition of vocabulary have demonstrated how few words are actually retained from those which are 'learned' or 'taught' by direct instruction. On the other hand, various researchers have concluded that for most proficient speakers of other languages, by far the largest part of their vocabulary has been 'caught' in the second way. This is also borne out by the reflections of speakers of other languages themselves.

It is surprising, therefore, that in recent years teachers have tended to become locked into the first of the two ways of providing opportunities for their learners to 'get' new vocabulary, at the expense of the second. Because there is a definite gap between what is 'taught' and what is 'learned', more attention needs to be paid to 'getting' vocabulary incidentally.

The aim of this book is to reflect critically, in the light of the above points, on the following issues:

- what vocabulary should be taught and how it should be taught;
- how vocabulary might be more focused on specific needs;
- techniques and strategies which are already in use;
- the extent to which some traditional language-learning activities might be revived to improve vocabulary learning;
- some idiosyncratic methods of rapidly expanding learners' stock of vocabulary;
- the additional options created by new technologies for effectively facilitating language acquisition by **absorption** within the classroom and home context;
- the contribution of the study of words to the **language awareness** and **cultural** aims of the National Curriculum;
- practical issues of teaching vocabulary in the light of the publication of the *Key Stage 3 MFL Framework* list of high-frequency words (DfES 2003).

The teacher's viewpoint

PLANNING

The problem with synonyms is that there aren't any! In everyday usage, these five words are generally more or less interchangeable. However, in the field of teaching vocabulary (as well as in other aspects of language teaching), three of these words have acquired very specific and distinct meanings. It is important for teachers to put them at the centre of their planning of schemes of work, of units of work and of individual lessons:

aims   **objectives**   **goals**

Although the coursebook can be a useful aid in planning, it should not be relied upon too heavily. The onus should be upon the teacher to make the connection between the objectives and goals of the current unit of work and the ways in which it is delivered to pupils.

It is for the above reasons that the following interpretation of aims, objectives and goals is offered here. Everything else in Part 2 of this book depends upon accepting these definitions.

Aims

can be expressed under four headings:

- communicative competence;
- language awareness;
- cultural awareness;
- general learning skills.

Objectives

are the specific ways in which the teacher gears his or her teaching towards one or more of the above aims. Objectives should be expressed in terms of what pupils should be able to do or should know by the end of a unit or by the end of a particular lesson.

Examples
- be able to express an opinion about a matter of personal interest (a function objective, linked to the communication aim);
- be able to write a few sentences about a recent experience (a grammatical objective, linked to the communication aim);
- know that there are three kinds of secondary school in Germany; or
- know that many French children think that wearing school uniforms is strange (knowledge objectives, linked to the cultural awareness aim);
- identify the general categories into which words fall (see *KS3 MFL Framework:* 'High-frequency words');
- use a dictionary to identify the gender of a noun (metalanguage objective, linked to the language-awareness aim);
- learn a text for a play (a language objective linked to general learning/memorising aim).

Goals

are what the teacher presents to pupils as a reason for a lesson or unit and should reflect the aims and objectives of the teacher. It is the **goals** that will mean most to pupils, so they should be **realistic, interesting, enjoyable, stimulating and challenging**.

Examples
- a project (e.g. individual, group or whole-class entry for a competition);
- a product (e.g. a wall display, making a cassette to send to a linked school);
- a process (e.g. reading or listening extensively for pleasure and/or to extend vocabulary acquisition);
- an experience (e.g. a trip abroad, or work experience, preparing to receive a group).

Most lessons should be presented within the context of these **goals**. Only the brightest, most well motivated pupils will react positively to the sort of language teaching which is directly linked to **aims** and **objectives**. This needs to be borne in mind when teachers are interpreting the *KS3 MFL Framework.*

What vocabulary should we include in a unit of work or a lesson?

The specific vocabulary to be 'learned' may come from:

- the coursebook;
- an exam specification;
- a frequency list which exists for all the commonly taught languages.

What often happens is that learning a list of words from one of the above sources is seen as an objective in itself. An inordinate amount of time can be spent on studying and practising a comprehensive list of vocabulary which is of doubtful use, or at least which has only limited use within one or two skill areas.

Before teaching pupils a particular selection of words, the teacher should really make judgements about these questions:

- What is the appropriate selection of vocabulary pupils will need to achieve the current **goal**?
- Will they need to 'know' this vocabulary for **receptive** purposes or for **productive** purposes?
- If receptive, does that mean understanding both the **spoken** words and the **written** words?
- If productive, will the ability to use the words in speaking **and** in writing be equally important?

In the initial planning stage a judgement should be made about the body of words to be learned in terms of the above questions. It is true that learning for one purpose probably helps learning for another and learning words for productive use will not be possible if they cannot first be used receptively. However, the teacher can be unduly influenced by the coursebook where the distinction may not necessarily be expressed.

For example, the topic of 'Weather' will generally be tackled from the angle of a traditional collection of verb phrases to be learned, as found in most courses (see opposite).

Admittedly, this is all very neat and tidy and it is certainly true that the aspect of vocabulary learning which involves thinking about how to organise words into groups is useful. However, young learners are seldom likely to be in situations where they will themselves need to use any of the words and phrases opposite, although much time is often wasted in their having to 'learn' them at school.

Under the topic of 'Weather', it would be more useful to start from the pupils' angle, with the question: 'Which words will I need to know to reach this particular goal?'.

Figure I

English	Deutsch	Español	Français
What's the weather like?	Wie ist das Wetter?	¿Qué tiempo hace?	Quel temps fait-il?
It's hot	Es ist warm	Hace calor	Il fait chaud
It's cold	Es ist kalt	Hace frío	Il fait froid
It's fine	Es ist sonnig	Hace buen tiempo	Il fait beau
It's poor weather	Es ist schlechtes Wetter	Hace mal tiempo	Il fait mauvais
It's raining	Es regnet	Llueve	Il pleut
It's snowing	Es schneit	Nieva	Il neige
It's hailing	Es hagelt	Graniza	Il grêle
It's freezing	Es friert	Hiela	Il gèle
It's foggy	Es ist nebelig	Hay niebla	Il fait du brouillard
It's windy	Es ist windig	Hace viento	Il fait du vent

The goal will be expressed in one or more of the following sorts of ways:

'By the end of this unit we will be able to:

a   understand a weather forecast on the television; or

b   understand a weather forecast on the radio; or

c   understand when our partner class is talking about the weather in their area (on tape, on video); or

d   understand a weather forecast in the newspaper; or

e   tell our partner class (on tape/in writing/by sending an e-mail) about what sort of weather they are likely to experience here when they visit us.'

When the pupil's goal has been agreed, pupil and teacher will need to choose an appropriate selection of words they will need by analysing actual weather forecasts used in a newspaper, on the radio, or on TV. Figure 2 illustrates some of the words and phrases they might find from these three sources and they will vary from language to language. You will see that they are totally different from all-purpose lists of phrasal expressions as are often taught under the topic 'Weather' (see Figure 1 above). The actual list from which pupils will work will only contain the vocabulary copied from the source which reflects their present goal, as outlined in **a–e** above.

Figure 2

English	Deutsch	Español	Français
rain	Regen	nuboso	pluie
showers	Sonnenschein	cielos cubiertos/ despejados	neige
sunshine	Nebel	tormentas	brouillard
sunny periods	Schnee	viento fuerte	tempêtes
fog	Kaltwetterfront	el norte/el sur/ el este/el oeste	vents forts/faibles
snow	Warmwetterfront	1–40 grados	soleil (sur la région parisienne/sur la moitié nord du pays)
wind	windig/stürmisch	bajo cero	les différentes regions
bright intervals	Hagel	soleado	vous aurez besoin d'un parapluie/d'un manteau/d'un gros pull
storms … in the north/south/ east/west	kalt/warm … im Süden … Norden … Osten … Westen	borrasca	
high/low pressure	hoher Luftdruck, niedriger Luftdruck	anticiclón	
higher/lower than normal temperatures		lluvias fuertes/débiles	

Furthermore, if the selection of vocabulary to be studied is made in this way, the learning can be much more focused and perhaps more effective than if the teacher tries to cover all four language skills with every new word.

For the goals **a–c** above, the words needed will be for **aural comprehension only**. The practical teaching consequence of this is that within this particular context there can be a much greater concentration on listening than when there is a perceived need to practise all four skills for all new vocabulary. The teacher may be able to set more demanding tasks and use more authentic material than is usually the case.

If the goal is as in **d** above, then the main thrust of the teaching at this stage would be the **reading** skill and, in particular, the ability to scan a text for information.

If the unit goal involved writing a letter or sending a tape to a partner, or sending an e-mail as in **e** above, the vocabulary needed would be different again. Figure 3 illustrates the sort of words and phrases pupils might come across if they analysed letters or tapes they had actually received from abroad. They would then be in a position to talk or write about the weather during their last holiday, or what it will be like when their visitors come next week and so on.

Figure 3

English	Deutsch	Español	Français
I hope it's not going to rain. It's always foggy at this time of the year. It should be fine when you arrive.	Wie war das Wetter? Das Wetter war (einfach) herrlich/angenehm/ furchtbar. Es war richtiges Frühlingswetter/ Sommerwetter/ Herbstwetter/ Winterwetter.	Hemos tenido un tiempo muy bueno, mucho sol aunque por la noche ha hecho frío. Espero que sigue este tiempo tan agradable.	Nous avons eu un hiver effroyable. Il a plu pendant tout le mois d'avril. J'espère qu'il fera beau pendant ton séjour.

If the specific vocabulary to be mastered is chosen with a particular written or spoken purpose in view, more intensive and demanding written or oral work can be done with learners than when the teacher is trying to cover a particular 'domain' in all four skills.

If we look at 'traditional' vocabulary lists from coursebooks or exam-board specifications we might draw similar conclusions as we did when we looked at the lists in Figure 1 above. What is the purpose, for example, of pupils 'learning' (which often means 'learning how to spell') all the parts of the body, all items of clothing or food, the names of all the pets, etc? How often does anyone have to use the written form of numbers (apart from 1–10)?

If vocabulary to be learned is targeted more accurately on a particular skill, as proposed above there will be more room in the classroom and at home for extensive reading and listening which are so often neglected for 'lack of time'. These are the activities which will provide learners with the opportunity to extend their vocabulary by subconscious acquisition rather than by 'learning' lists.

It could rightly be argued that what is suggested in terms of a rethink in attitudes towards lists of vocabulary to be learnt is an overwhelming task and not one for the individual teacher. However, the proposal here is more modest: simply to reduce the amount of time spent on learning lists, in order to allow more time for other things. For those who might wish to pursue the idea of developing a critical attitude towards lists, there is a suggestion on p112 about using post-16 learners in the process.

'LEARN THE NEW VOCABULARY FOR HOMEWORK'

It is certainly each teacher's prerogative to use whatever tools, strategies or activities have been found to work – and setting vocabulary learning as a homework task is certainly one of the traditional 'things to do' when teaching languages. However, the complaint is often to be heard that 'they won't/don't do their homework, particularly when it's learning' so it is perhaps worthwhile discussing the reasons for this and reassessing whether the activity is useful and, if so, whether it can be made more effective. If the instruction 'learn the new vocabulary for homework' is to have productive results in language learning, it is worth considering our **objectives** when we give the instruction and then to make sure that the pupils have the same perception and understanding of what is required.

Learning vocabulary for homework may be appropriate in schools where the tradition of homework is well established and the teacher can be sure that an instruction to 'learn the new words for homework' will be understood:

- the teacher will have taught the skills of memorising (and will remind them before each 'learning' homework how to go about it (see Chapter 10, p110);
- he or she will have a clear picture of the way in which the new words fit into his or her objectives and scheme of work and will make sure that the pupils see the learning in terms of the current unit **goal**;
- the teacher will be clear in his or her own mind whether the vocabulary to be learned will be needed for receptive or productive use.

When the learning has been undertaken, the teacher needs to weigh up the advantage of testing (just to show whether or not pupils have done what they were told) against the time taken for the test, which might be more effectively spent on practising, reinforcing and using the new words in context.

If the learning is followed by a test, the test should reflect the objectives of the teacher and should not automatically be a question of pupils having to supply target-language equivalents, correctly spelt, of English words.

TESTING EACH OTHER

An alternative to the written test is a regular five-minute session where the pupils test each other orally in pairs (see Appendix A: 'Groupwork and pairwork'). If it is pointed out to pupils that one of the best ways of learning is by teaching, both sides of the testing–tested partnerships will have motivation to get on with the job. The sense that people feel when faced with a test is not that their knowledge is being checked, but that they are being tested as people. When pair-testing is going on there can be a real sense of helping each other to learn.

ASSESSMENT

Whether testing is by the teacher or by peers, pupils need to learn from their errors. It is at this stage that the teacher may wish to use a whole–class brainstorm, to reassess how some pupils have achieved the relevant task and others have not.

If the 'Tip of the day' suggestion has been used (see Chapter 10), this would be a suitable stage to 'brainstorm' the class about whether or not the tip worked for them. They might then rewrite it in terms of the experience of the most successful members of the class. It is when pupils have had a chance to try the teacher's suggestions for learning that they can find out for themselves how best to go about a particular task.

RE-TESTING

If the regular process of learning, testing, assessment and feedback is followed, the next step will be to give pupils a further opportunity to reinforce the new vocabulary, before using it to achieve the current **goal**.

This is probably the most delicate stage from the teacher's point of view, for he or she has to balance the needs of those who have already learned the new vocabulary, those who have not and those in between. It could be at this stage that alternative ways of reinforcement might be introduced, as suggested below.

ALTERNATIVES TO 'LEARN THE NEW WORDS FOR HOMEWORK'

There are more specific homework tasks for reinforcing new vocabulary which pupils find more motivating than the vague **'learn-for-a-test'** approach. If the teacher has decided that the emphasis for a particular group of words must be on the form of the words, or **spelling**, the following **strategies for reinforcing** them are worth considering. The principles can be adapted for use with near-beginners or advanced learners.

- Write sentences, each including one of the new words, in such a way as to show the meaning of the word. (In Classic Pathfinder 1: *You speak, they speak* (Jones, Halliwell and Holmes 2002), Bernardette Holmes suggests that this could also be a spoken activity. Learners would memorise and record each word within a sentence or short paragraph which they create for themselves.)
- On a sheet of paper write a sentence using each of the new words. Put the new words in pencil. When you have finished, rub out the 'new' words and we will see if others in the class can put in the correct words tomorrow. (You will need to remember what you have put, so that you can check what other people think!)
- Write a definition of each of the new words.
- Write some anagrams which we will try on each other tomorrow. You will need to be able to judge whether or not your friends get the right answer!
- Write a word-search including the new words. We will try this on other people within the next few days.

In all these cases, the focus is on learning the **form** or **spelling** of the words which, as we have seen, is not always the teacher's objective. When it is, however:

- each of the suggested tasks has a purpose which pupils can see and is likely to be more motivating than a simple instruction to 'learn the new words for homework';
- all of them require a particular effort of thought, rather than simple memorising.

The pupil's viewpoint

Before any **meaningful** learning will take place, the pupil needs to know the answers to the following five questions:

■ 'WHY DO I NEED TO LEARN THESE PARTICULAR WORDS?'

In the first column are the answers he or she may be given or may deduce from the teacher's attitude. In the second column are the ways the cynical, or over-loaded pupil might see it and in the third column is a comment for reflection.

Why learn these words?	A reasonable reaction	Food for thought
The teacher says so.	I will do as I'm told: I have faith in what the teacher says.	*An admirable sentiment, but alas not universal!*
Research suggests that we need to hear/see new words up to twelve times before we remember them.	Well, I'll never learn this language then!	*Perhaps this is one of those pieces of information which is best kept to ourselves and* **remembered in our planning***?*
They are in the book.	I'm not interested. Books are boring.	*Has the writer of the coursebook hit the right level for the pupils in terms of* **realism**, **interest**, **fun**, **intellectual challenge and stimulation***?*
They are in the GCSE specification.	The GCSE is years away. **or** I'm fed up hearing about the GCSE.	*Is it the teacher's job to add to the anxiety about exams and the sense of boredom and tiredness they can create?*

Table continued overleaf

Why learn these words?	A reasonable reaction	Food for thought
These are 'general-purpose' words; they are needed for everything we want to say or write or understand in the foreign language.	Such words will be met frequently anyway, so what is so special about learning them at home instead of in class?	*Yes, perhaps more focused learning, listening or reading would be a better use of their time. Beware of thinking of the 'high-frequency words' from the KS3 MFL Framework as a list to be 'learned'!*
These words will be necessary if we are to achieve (the goal) of this lesson or unit.	An excellent reason to spend some time on **learning** them.	*If we bear in mind the needs of the present **goal**, which of the four skills do we need to practise? So how should we learn the new words? (See next section)*

'WHAT DO YOU MEAN, LEARN?'

On the left are the teacher's possible objectives. On the right are points for reflection:

Objective	Can this be achieved by a 'learning' homework?
To recognise the words when you see them.	*Yes. Are the pupils aware that this is the teacher's only objective? Do they know how to go about learning for this purpose?*
To recognise the words when you hear them.	*Maybe (if they have been well practised in class, first). Perhaps the more able can do this by the end of the lesson anyway. Will the less well motivated spend the time wisely?*
To use the words to talk about … (whatever is the current **goal**).	*Not unless they have already started along this road in class.*
To use them when you write about … (the current **goal**).	
To be able to translate from English into the target language.	*Well, yes, but is this really our objective when we profess to be training pupils to think in the target language? Because this is the easiest way of testing lists of words to be learned, it has unfortunately become the commonest procedure.*
All the above, or just to fulfil the requirement to set homework.	*Not a chance! The teacher's objectives need to be much more carefully focused than this.*

'How do we learn?'

This is not a question which will often be posed by young learners, but experience shows that it is a matter on which they need guidance if their learning is to be effective. In the following chapters there are suggestions about various ways of learning vocabulary and, whatever strategies are used by teachers, they will be more effective if pupils are given reasons for learning. Suffice it here to say that if a 'learning vocabulary' homework is deemed suitable for a particular selection of words:

- the **need** for it should be made explicit (i.e. the pupils' need, in terms of the current **goal**);
- the exact **focus** of the learning should to be specified (are they learning for receptive use or productive use?);
- the **way to go about** the learning will be explained (see Chapter 10 and Part 1: Chapter 5);
- the follow-up (a test or some other task) will reflect both the **objectives** and **the way pupils have learned**.

A way of helping learners understand the **need** and **focus** for 'learning' a particular group of words is to ask them 'How do you know a word?' (Examples of the way in which this strategy can be developed are included on the ILIAD CD-ROM, produced by the Open University 2002.)

'How will we be tested on the learning homework?'

It seems to be axiomatic that what has been learned for homework must be tested. So pupils will have been taught to expect a test and it often simply takes the form of a series of words in English for the pupil to write the equivalents in the target language. It is worth remembering here that the test should accurately reflect what has been learned, so that the English-into-the-target-language test would only be valid when the goal of the unit involved **translation** (see 'What do you mean, learn?' above).

'Why do we need a test?'

It might be argued, with some justification, that if the teacher does not test, the pupils will not do the task. However, it is also necessary to weigh up the value of the test and the time it takes against the time needed for other reinforcement activities which might be more important in the learning cycle.

When the above points have been debated, the teacher may still see the test as necessary in some circumstances. If that is the case, there are three other forms of testing which might be considered more appropriate, in reflecting the objective(s) of setting such homework, than the simple translation technique:

1   The teacher uses the same stimuli as in the initial presentation of the words (real objects, pictures, symbols or mime). The instruction is then to write the word in the target language.

2   The teacher presents the stimulus but the response is **oral** rather than written. This may be more appropriate than a written test, if the words are to be used for a spoken task, such as a tape-recording or video to be sent to a partnership school.

3   A cloze test in which the gaps are the words learned for homework. (The words are supplied or not, depending on the teacher's objectives.) This would be appropriate if written material (a letter or a report) was the goal of the unit.

NB If a test on vocabulary learned for homework is considered important, it should be made clear to pupils that this is a link in the chain of learning. It is not just a way of finding out whether or not they have 'done their homework'! Whether a test is traditional or peer-based, as outlined in Chapter 1, it is not an end in itself. Immediate feedback and follow-up remedial work is essential if the test is to achieve anything.

3   The vocabulary notebook

Is it necessary for pupils to keep a vocabulary notebook?

Opinion is divided about the value of the vocabulary notebook and it is not the purpose of this chapter to be dogmatic on the subject. It is perhaps a matter which is best discussed at departmental level and then left to the individual teacher to make a decision for each class. The following notes are offered as a framework for discussion.

Pros	Cons
The proven efficacy of **organised** learning. There is some evidence to suggest that memory is assisted by sorting words into lists, according to different parts of speech.	Particularly with children, the time taken for keeping a vocabulary book has to be balanced against all the other important activities. (Will there still be time for independent reading and listening as well as working on the vocabulary books?)
Through the notebook pupils can be taught to think about the **function** of the word rather than just the **form**, or how it is spelt.	What they write must be **accurate** or they will be learning from a faulty model. So frequent checking and correcting is essential. Has the teacher enough time?
Vocabulary growth is somewhat slowed by 'forgetting'. Almost half the new words 'learned' seem to get lost.	Does keeping a vocabulary notebook create a 'word-for-word' mentality?
The vocabulary book serves as a focus for regular revision.	Does it create 'translation' thinking when we hope to encourage pupils to think in the target language?

If a notebook is kept what should go into it?

When the above issues have been considered, it may well be decided that the more able language learners could benefit from keeping vocabulary notebooks. In this case, it would be worthwhile planning in advance how pupils will be taught to compile and use them.

The simplest course of action is for the teacher to get the pupils to copy down whatever crops up. However, if the vocabulary to be included is what is already in the coursebook, there is little to be added by pupils simply copying down the new words. It is perhaps better to group the new vocabulary according to broad categories of high-frequency words, as outlined in the *Framework KS3 MFL* under 'Words 7W'.

The notebook can be roughly divided into three main sections at the planning stage:

* domains such as family and home, school/classroom, routines, pastimes, meeting and greeting, daily life here and in the foreign country;
* grammatical function (verbs, nouns, pronouns, prepositions, adverbs, interrogatives, connectives, etc);
* classroom talk (subdivided into teacher instructions and pupil requests).

SIMPLE RULES FOR KEEPING THE NOTEBOOK

It is worthwhile spending a little time at the beginning of the year and at intervals throughout the course on teaching pupils how to organise their notebooks. Then they need to be given simple instructions about what goes into them.

* The quickest entry is the target-language word plus the English. However, this does have the drawback of being contrary to the spirit of target-language teaching and can lead to a word-for-word translation mentality. A compromise which some teachers use is to have the English written in pencil, to be erased as soon as it is known, thus signalling that the English is just a prop for initial understanding.
* The target-language word plus a graphic (picture, symbol, icon): for younger learners this is the arrangement most consistent with target-language teaching, but it has the disadvantage that it takes pupils time to draw pictures and the drawings usually become more important than the words. Furthermore, not all meanings can be represented in this way.

For more advanced learners, there are two other possible sorts of entry, which may be slower but more useful:

* the new word plus a synonym (and/or antonym);
* the target-language word with a meaningful target-language definition.

Either of these latter systems of keeping a vocabulary notebook, or a combination of the two, can be linked to some work with monolingual dictionaries and/or a thesaurus. Time spent on such activities is an invaluable way of teaching learners to get beyond the initial 'meaning' of words (see Chapter 8).

What can be stated unequivocally is that when vocabulary notebooks **are** kept, the teacher will need to check that what goes into them is **accurate** and in accordance with the **rules** which he or she lays down, for instance:

- nouns must always appear with an article (or possessive adjective);
- nouns should be grouped together according to gender (denoted by colour-coding or by the position of each gender on the page);
- verbs should be accompanied by the appropriate tag (probably the infinitive, but maybe the relevant pronoun).

If vocabulary notebooks are considered necessary, they will only be effective if pupils are trained to use them regularly:

- as the first point of reference;
- to test each other;
- to analyse newly acquired vocabulary.

4   Playing games: A waste of time?

'I liked French in the first two or three years —
but when we started to . . .
     . . . do grammar
or) . . . prepare for the GCSE
or) . . . just do writing)   . . . I hated it.'

'I don't like German
because all you do is
play games.'

These two apparently contradictory types of comment may be two sides of the same coin. There is certainly something to be said for playing games purely for fun, particularly in the early stages of introducing children to a new language. The proliferation of language teaching in primary schools in recent years and the sort of remarks quoted above bear witness to children's enjoyment of this aspect of language learning. However, to play games **just for fun** or to allow games to monopolise language learning in the classroom can be wasteful of valuable time. The second remark above suggests that serious pupils can become irritated by what they see as pointless activities when all other influences in their lives are telling them to work hard and 'get good results'.

What is needed is a more balanced approach to word-games throughout KS3 and KS4. It helps the more serious minded to accept the idea of playing games if they are 'let into the secret' about the contribution of a particular game to the goal of the moment. The pupils who just like playing games because it is easy and enjoyable can also benefit by being given reasons which go beyond immediate gratification. (The idea of 'letting pupils into the secrets' is further developed in Chapter 10).

The field of English as a Foreign Language has provided a wealth of suggestions of games to play in teaching English and some of these have filtered into MFL teaching. What is not always made explicit is the extent to which these games contribute to a particular objective.

It is worthwhile looking at the commonest of the word-games to see how they can be used to fit what we know about ways of learning vocabulary.

The following three principles are fundamental to whether or not we choose a particular word-game and, more importantly, how we play it:

- words are best learned and practised in a context;
- the majority of words which we learn are not actually taught, but imbibed as a result of doing something else;
- there will only be a point to the game if the vocabulary content is chosen with a view to the particular **goal** of a unit of work and if the game is modified to use the words appropriately (i.e. receptively or actively, for reading or for hearing).

When the above principles are borne in mind as the reason for playing a particular game and attention is drawn to them, word-games can have a particular role to play in teaching vocabulary.

VARIATIONS ON 'PELMANISM' (played in pairs)

A series of pairs of cards are laid face down in random order. Players take it in turn to turn over two cards and keep the pair if they match.

1 Half the cards have the target-language word and half the English word.

When we are trying to get learners to think in the foreign language it is not easy to justify this variation in mainstream teaching. However, for those with special learning needs, developing **language awareness** is one of the most important reasons for MFL learning. Pupils whose recognition of English word-forms is very elementary may therefore benefit from playing this variation of 'Pelmanism'.

2 Half the cards have the target-language word and half a picture or symbol.

This works well for reinforcing simple **recognition** of the written form, if that is what is appropriate for the particular selection of words being used for the game.

3 All cards have picture pairs with no words, such as those for young English children, where the game involves **saying** the words (*zwei Hünder, dos perros, deux chiens*, etc).

This is a useful game where the **goal** of the unit of work is something like: 'We are going to send a tape to our partner class, telling them about …' This variation is a way of focusing on **speaking**. Of course, there needs to be a clear instruction about how to proceed and they do need to be monitored. Otherwise, they will play the game in English!

4 Target-language word and a common 'twin'. The content of the cards can be adapted for playing at any level from complete beginners to very advanced. Sets of words can be created using the following types of 'twinning':

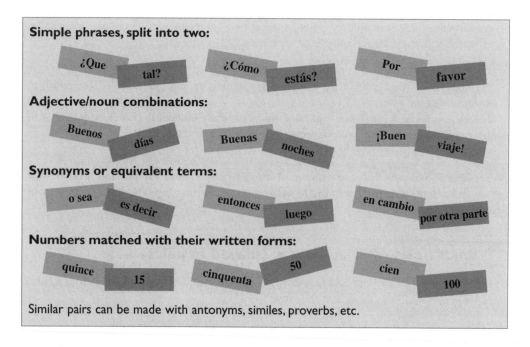

Simple phrases, split into two:

¿Qué · tal?

¿Cómo · estás?

Por · favor

Adjective/noun combinations:

Buenos · días

Buenas · noches

¡Buen · viaje!

Synonyms or equivalent terms:

o sea · es decir

entonces · luego

en cambio · por otra parte

Numbers matched with their written forms:

quince · 15

cinquenta · 50

cien · 100

Similar pairs can be made with antonyms, similes, proverbs, etc.

Playing a game of this sort for five minutes could be more valuable than sending pupils away to 'learn the numbers' for homework. With numbers, the most important skills are listening and speaking and, to a lesser degree, reading. The ability to **spell** numbers is only needed, possibly, for letter-writing (numbers 1–10) and yet much time is often wasted on demanding that pupils learn how to do this.

An additional way of making the most of 'pelmanism' is for pupils to make the cards for homework. Different groups in the class are given different topic areas for which to make sets of cards. They then 'play' the game with each other's sets in class. Getting them to **create the cards for themselves** is not only helpful in terms of saving the teacher's time, but it is also a way of getting pupils to think about which words go together and getting them to copy accurately!

◼ 'BINGO'/'LOTTO' (played as a whole class)

Played in its traditional form this is an excellent game for practising hearing and understanding numbers. It can easily be graded in difficulty to suit the level of the learner:

'On your blank grid write down any nine numbers between 1 and 10', or 'any number between 30 and 60', or 'Write down five numbers each including a 5 or each including a 4', etc. (Of course, the teacher may wish to use target language for these instructions.)

'Bingo'/'Lotto' can also be a useful way of practising those words which are more likely to be needed for the receptive skills than the productive skills. In this case, the words would be printed on the 'Bingo' grid instead of numbers.

'NOUGHTS AND CROSSES' (whole-class team game, played on the board)

Virtually any set of vocabulary can be practised and there can be incentives to make pupils think of **combinations of words** or **words in context** built into the rules, for example:

- practising talking about the family: 'You must use *mon/ma* or *mes* to get a nought or a cross: *mon père, ma mère, mes parents*';
- practising talking about school subjects: 'You must use a verb to get a nought or a cross: *habla inglés, estudiamos matemáticas, Señor Jones enseña la historia*';
- practising prepositions: 'You must give a whole sentence, including the preposition to get a nought or a cross: *Sie kommt aus Bremen. Die Bank ist gegenüber dem Supermarkt*'.

ANAGRAMS (in pairs or as a whole-class teamgame, played on the board)

These are a well-tried way of focusing on the spelling of new words. They should be words that pupils have already met and practised in the spoken form and they should be used in context **before** and **after** playing the game. There is little point in anagrams unless the words concerned are those which learners will need frequently for **writing** (see Chapter 1 and *KS3 MFL Framework* 'High-frequency words').

Asking pupils to **write anagrams themselves** to try on their classmates is an equally valuable activity, particularly if they are told that they will not have the words in front of them when they are checking the results!

WORD SEARCHES (individually or in pairs)

Because word searches are popular with children and because they keep them quiet, they are often allowed to take more time than they are worth. However, getting pupils to make up their **own** word searches to try out on each other is an excellent way of encouraging accurate copying for an obvious purpose. When the other pupils actually do these searches they should be instructed to write down the words they find, rather than just to put a line through them.

CROSSWORDS (individually or in pairs)

These can be a very useful way of reinforcing vocabulary for the more able language learners. They are also popular with people of any age. They do have the advantage of making the learner think, particularly when the clues are also in the target language.

NB If the teacher has to compile the crosswords him- or herself, it is easier to produce the sort of crossword which does not have to fit into a square. There are many programs which will assist in this task, e.g. *Teacher's Pet* and *TaskMagic*.

I WENT TO MARKET, AND I BOUGHT SOME BANANAS ... (best played in groups, rather than with the whole class)

Each individual repeats the previous statement and adds an item of his or her own. The effort of memory creates an immediate purpose for the activity. There is an infinite number of ways in which this game can be adapted for practising vocabulary needed for **listening** and **speaking goals**. ('My grandmother went to the doctor's because she had earache, backache ...', 'We went to school and we took our pens, our pencils ...', 'I went to my friend's house to listen to a new album, to watch a new DVD...', etc.)

CRACKING CODES AND SOLVING PUZZLES (individually or in pairs)

There are books of codes to crack and puzzles to solve available commercially. They may have some entertainment value, if little else. However, getting pupils **to write their own codes** for their partners to crack, using recently encountered vocabulary, has the same advantage as composing anagrams. If pupils are in a computer club at school, or if they have their own computer at home, they can easily be persuaded to do this sort of thing as an alternative to playing games! (see Chapter 8).

GAMES ON THEIR FEET

In addition to using the above suggestions, teachers might wish to explore the various imaginative suggestions for playing games in Classic Pathfinder 3: *Inspiring performance* (Hamilton, McLeod and Fawkes 2003). In Chapter 3: 'Focus on drama', for instance, there are memory games which can be used to reinforce vocabulary acquisition by constant repetition and movement games where actions accompanying language can help subconscious absorption of vocabulary (see my Introduction, 'Words which are "caught"'). The principles of establishing the value of a particular game in achieving the current **goal** will, of course, still apply.

5   The old skills revisited

Effective vocabulary teaching involves:

- introducing new words in **a context**;
- gearing the context to **the needs** and **interests** of the learner;
- creating opportunities for **frequent practice**;
- making opportunities for learners to **encounter new words incidentally**.

Language teachers will have fairly strong views about what has contributed to their own proficiency in the language(s) they teach. Most people will feel they have benefited from and, indeed, sometimes enjoyed most of the following seven language learning activities:

- extended listening;
- translation from the target language;
- translation into the target language (sometimes referred to as 'prose');
- extended reading;
- summarising;
- dictation;
- transcription.

Because all these activies have played a part in their own language acquisition, teachers may have mixed feelings about not including them in their teaching today. They may feel that some of these activities are forbidden by the 'new orthodoxy' or excluded by the time taken to fulfil the requirements of the National Curriculum or the *KS3 MFL Framework*. This may be a suitable point at which to reconsider the extent to which any or all the above techniques can be beneficial in developing vocabulary in a meaningful way.

Changing fashions in language teaching have meant that sometimes very important aspects of language provision have been forced out by changes in emphasis. The somewhat limited interpretation of 'communicative language teaching', with its emphasis on spoken negotiation, has indeed improved learners' ability to be confident in getting what they want by **speaking**. What has been lost in the process is the development of the receptive skills, which many learners used to find easier to acquire!

LISTENING

Use of the target language by the teacher

One of the threads running through the National Curriculum has been the importance of getting pupils to accept the foreign language as the normal means of communication in the classroom. In recent years, many language teachers have become proficient in achieving this. New vocabulary is usually introduced or explained by the techniques of using pictures (either carefully prepared or improvised on the spot), by using mime, by giving synonyms and antonyms, by definitions in the target language, etc. Many teachers are also aware of the difference between the written and the spoken language and may therefore choose to explain the meaning of a heard word by simply writing it on the board. This development in target-language teaching is certainly one of the best ways in the classroom context of ensuring that frequently needed vocabulary is heard often enough to become fixed. (Readers can find a comprehensive treatment of the subject of target-language teaching in Classic Pathfinder 1: *You speak, they speak* by Jones, Halliwell and Holmes 2002).

The target language as a medium for learning something else

The most effective way of encountering words incidentally is clearly through living for a period in one of the countries where the target language is spoken. However, this is not an option for the majority of our learners, although the school visit abroad can be a valuable substitute. (The importance of giving pupils an opportunity for a visit abroad, as listed among the 40 'opportunities' in the National Curriculum programmes of study, is one which should be taken seriously by all schools. Such a visit does indeed contribute to vocabulary extension and language enhancement, although the main possibilities for such a visit will be in the field of cultural awareness.) Some people would say that from the point of view of vocabulary acquisition an equally useful strategy is to teach another subject in the target language, such as is commonly done in Canada and some international schools in Europe. There are certainly those who are planning to increase the amount of teaching of other subjects through the medium of the foreign language and it is something which can be done on a small scale from quite an early age, even within the ordinary classroom. If the subject matter is not entirely unfamiliar to the learners (elementary scientific experiments, easy sums, basic Geography or History, for example) and is well supported by visuals, young learners can get a sense of achievement and confidence in understanding the foreign language, at the same time as acquiring words by hearing them in context. A growing number of UK schools are involved in such Content and Language Integrated Learning (CLIL).

Widening the choice of materials

The third way of ensuring that learners have the opportunity to enrich their vocabulary by **incidental encounter** is by the teachers providing learners with a variety of listening material in addition to what is needed for the initial presentation of selected new vocabulary. There is much excellent recorded listening material accompanying coursebooks and the advantages of using this material for regular listening practice in the classroom are generally agreed. However, if it can be accepted that acquiring vocabulary is best done incidentally while doing something else (talking to native speakers, listening and reading) the teacher does need to provide opportunities at all levels for listening which goes beyond what is currently the norm.

Successful whole-class listening

In addition to commercial recordings, some teachers build up a stock of home-made materials which can be valuable resources for different levels of learners. Recordings of people known to the pupils, even if not technically perfect, can have a greater impact on learners than course material, which is often presented like any other classroom exercise. (For teachers who have not yet tried creating their own listening materials there are some suggestions in Appendix B.)

Whatever material is used, the most productive listening takes place when the four following principles are observed.

- Listening in the classroom is not always just for testing, but it often looks like that to learners. The teacher should, ideally, avoid saying:

  'Now we're going to do a listening comprehension' or 'Here's a listening test'.

- Listening as a teaching strategy is more effective when this approach is used:

  'Now let's all listen to these (target-language) people speaking about ...'

- Pupils are more likely to make the effort if they see the teacher listening as well (and sometimes not quite hearing).

- The activity will be more productive in terms of vocabulary acquisition if pupils understand that the teacher is teaching them how to listen, rather than just judging them.

READING

Ideally, each MFL classroom should have its own mini-library (or Reading Box), containing a wide selection of reading material. The books in it should be presented in a variety of styles and look very different from the coursebook which is sometimes the only source of reading material a child ever sees. There should be simplified historical and fictional material, sheets of cartoons, jokes, strange facts, etc. Magazines designed for various ages have long been produced by publishers such as Mary Glasgow Magazines, but there is also so much available now that teachers (or pupils themselves) can create selections downloaded from the Internet.

The Reading Box should not be something which gathers dust and becomes a box full of tatters, but a responsible pupil can become the 'librarian' and keep it tidy. Pupils should not only have access to such material, but:

- they should be taught **how** to read (see Chapter 10 and Part 1, Chapter 3);
- they should be given **time** in class and for homework to use the reading material;
- they should be **monitored** to check that they are doing the job.

(Some teachers use a simple pro-forma for pupils to fill in when they have completed each reading task – rather than giving them a list of questions in English. Another technique is simply to ask pupils to tell the teacher, or the whole class, what it was about and what they thought of it.)

At the post-16 stage, there are clearly many more possibilities of providing a wide range of reading materials. The excellent magazines and tapes published by Authentik, available in several languages, are ideal from both points of view. There are various possible ways of using the press and radio extracts which are included, but one of the best ways is to give pupils the whole mgazine and tape to study over a period of time (say, a holiday period) possibly with instructions to concentrate on certain items. This is then followed by a test, written and aural, using the sorts of techniques suggested in the *feuille de travail* provided by the publishers or testing types which are peculiar to the exam board. If this becomes a regular activity during an advanced course there is really no need for them to study lists of words out of context as sometimes happens at present.

TRANSLATION FROM THE TARGET LANGUAGE

The reason why translation became unfashionable was that it approached language learning from an angle which actually interfered with acquiring the skill of thinking in the language and if it was begun too early it encouraged the view that language was only real if it was our own language. Furthermore, it was a hard exercise which involved a lot of thinking and research in dictionaries. For the last reason and because the art of translation does demand precise analysis of words in context, it is still irreplaceable as a skill to be practised at a high level of language study. For example, translation from the target language into English is an excellent activity for teachers themselves to continue practising to keep their own proficiency well honed.

As far as translating every word newly heard or read into English is concerned, the development of target-language teaching has shown that this is simply not necessary and interferes with the direct association of meaning with words. However, teachers will still make the judgement that sometimes a translation into English is the quickest way of explaining a new word. This is not something they should feel guilty about, but they should make a point of supporting the translation with one of the other techniques for presentation and should put the word into a context as quickly as possible. Then the initial use of the English as a prop will only be needed once.

At the post-16 stage a little free translation to be undertaken as an occasional exercise is a valuable way of getting learners to think about precise meanings of words in particular contexts. However, to have all new texts translated into English, 'just to be sure they really understand them' is ill-advised, encouraging a translation view of language which runs counter to the main aim of helping learners to think **in the language**.

TRANSLATION INTO THE TARGET LANGUAGE

At a level somewhere beyond A level, translating into the target language can be a valuable exercise in developing precise understanding of both languages. There would appear to be no justification for beginners and intermediate learners to translate from their mother tongue. Even if the **goal** of the moment is to speak or write about an aspect of their own lives (in a communication with their correspondents), the preparation is best done by their writing a few notes **in the target language**, rather than preparing in English first.

SUMMARISING

This is one of the best approaches to the reinforcement of vocabulary – and it does not have to be left for more advanced learners. It can be done as soon as pupils are able to understand and use the third person of the commonest verbs in the past.

- The teacher speaks to the class as a whole, along these lines:
- either 'At the weekend … (or Yesterday evening … or During the holidays …) I went to … and …';
- or else the teacher recounts a previously known story, maybe illustrating it with sketches or mime at the same time (*Hansel and Gretel* goes down well with thirteen and fourteen year-olds, if the gruesome side is emphasised!);
- or (at KS4) recounts a real story from the news.
- The pupils are asked to note key-words (or the teacher may choose to identify them, writing them on the board as he or she speaks).
- The pupils then have to retell the story (to the whole class or in pairs – see Appendix B) using their own words.

The same technique can be used for reinforcing new vocabulary using a written text. Instead of jotting down keywords, learners can be asked to find a suitable title, or a series of headings, to use as the basis for producing a summary in their own words.

 ## DICTATION

When the emphasis in language learning was on written accuracy, the formal dictation used to play a prominent part in developing that accuracy. With the advent of a more communicatively based approach, it was realised that the time taken to achieve competence in this purely academic skill was out of all proportion to its usefulness in terms of real language usage.

However, there are occasions when reasonable written accuracy is what is needed to achieve a particular **goal**. There is little point in pupils making wall displays or writing to correspondents if what they write is not accurate. To say that they can get an A* in the GCSE without being completely accurate is irrelevant in terms of the professed aims and objectives of teaching languages!

It is, then, in the field of written accuracy that the dictation of individual words or phrases can be a useful way of practising new vocabulary, providing always that the vocabulary has been identified as necessary for **written expression.**

Dictation can also be a helpful teaching device to practise the changes in sub-elements of vocabulary (verb endings, case endings, silent letters, etc).

TRANSCRIPTION

This is a development of the traditional dictation and one which is worth mentioning at this stage. Although the transcription is probably inappropriate for pre-16 learners, it is a most successful exercise for more advanced students as well as for teachers wishing to hone their own language skills in a second language. Transcription differs from dictation in that the stimulus consists of the recording of a passage of real spoken language, as opposed to the teacher's slow reading, as in a dictation. The student can listen as often as necessary and may even use a dictionary to assist him or her in the task.

Apart from its intrinsic use in extending and reinforcing vocabulary, this is also a skill which teachers of advanced students find particularly useful in creating a written version of a piece of listening material, for further exploitation and study.

For this purpose, recordings from sound radio are generally superior to video recordings where the pictures tend to interfere with concentration. Teachers of French and German may wish to consult **www.wotsat.com** where you can go to a wide selection of programmes by clicking on 'radio links'. Teachers of Spanish will find the main Spanish radio stations at **www.rne.es/envivo.htm**.

6   Verbs are words, too

Whether we consider verbs as an element in the grammatical structure of a language or whether we look upon them as items of vocabulary is not a matter which needs to be debated here. However, a consideration of the ways of teaching and learning verbs does fit neatly into this book. The practical difference between learning, say, a noun and a verb lies in the multiplicity of different forms that the verb has in the commonly taught languages. It is this considerable body of words and 'sub-words' which can cause such confusion and despair among learners.

In traditional grammar-translation teaching, verbs were taught as though they had a life of their own. Verbs were introduced in strict rotation: present tense (regular, irregular, interrogative, imperative, negative interrogative, negative imperatives), future tenses, past tenses and so on. And all these forms were given names and learned in a particular order (first-person singular, second-person singular …). The tidy mind of the grammatically motivated teacher had no bounds. Even long-since obsolete forms were taught to all learners because they completed the jigsaw and somehow the job did not seem complete without them. The result of this approach was a very thorough understanding of verbs by the most able language learners but it was also the source of complete confusion for the majority and it certainly did not lead to the oral fluency of any of them.

'Communicative language teaching' has led some teachers to take the completely opposite line in teaching verbs: in the most extreme cases, verbs are taught as items of vocabulary like any other parts of speech, whenever they occur, or when the need arises to fulfil a particular task. This approach ignores the tremendous potential of drawing attention to the patterns which exist and using these patterns as an aid to acquiring an extensive stock of verbs.

The compromise position adopted by many teachers is as follows:

- teach new verb forms from the point of view of the need of the moment (which verbs or parts of verbs you will need in order to achieve the current **goal**);
- define the words as they crop up in the course of reading or listening (or, in an ideal world, as they are being used to teach another subject);
- at an appropriate stage, take a group of parts of the verb and draw attention to the pattern with other verbs (formation, regularities, irregularities);
- practise the new verbs/parts of verbs in **drills** and in a **realistic context**;
- set tasks which involve using them orally and possibly in writing, in ways which are realistic and will aid recall;

- continue drilling and using verbs in context at frequent intervals and with different topic areas;
- remember that 'grammar teaching' fell out of fashion because teachers found that grammatical **jargon** was confusing to the majority of young learners.

As an introduction to the imperfect tense, for example, pupils might hear people talking about life in the past or see some writing about what things used to be like. Then the following goal could be specified:

> *'We're going to ask some senior citizens what life was like when they were young, then we're going to tell our partners in [target-language country] what we have found out. Their teachers are going to organise the same sort of report and then we'll compare life here with life there.'*

The next step will be to go to the text which was initially read or heard fairly superficially for interest or information. This time, the tense in question will be examined and rules for formation specified. Some practice will naturally follow.

This sequence may be sufficient for the learners to tackle the particular task in hand, but if the new tense is to become part of their permanent language baggage it will need to be **over-learned**.

It is at this stage that **drilling** will be most useful. Apart from those who have learned a second language by total immersion, most proficient foreign language speakers will confess to the need for **verb practice** or **drilling**.

Drilling need not necessarily be a chore for learners, but if they are actually to enjoy the experience it needs to be kept to **very frequent short bursts** and presented in terms they can appreciate:

- professional sportspeople need to continue to practise the basic skills long after becoming proficient at their sport;
- people go jogging or do aerobics to keep in trim;
- actors exercise in the gym and need to practise their lines long after they think they know them;
- musicians practise their scales even when they are expert concert performers;
- **speakers of foreign languages need to keep practising their verbs**.

Drills are successful if they are done at high-speed with a whole class by the teacher, but there are additional advantages if learners are trained to work in pairs (see Appendix A). The sort of verb drills which are most useful are those which spring from actual speech patterns:

1 *Aimes-tu ...? Oui, j'aime ... Non, je n'aime pas ...*
   Aimes-tu les escargots? Oui, j'aime les escargots. Non, je n'aime pas les escargots.
2 *Tomber. Je ...? Il ...?* (followed, on different occasions, by other common regular -er verbs, followed by -ir verbs, followed by irregulars, etc).
3 As for **2** but using the English for the stimulus.

NB The ability to chant a paradigm '*ich bin, du bist, er/sie/es ...*' is not very useful. Learning a list of infinitives, before the use of the infinitive is understood or needed and before learners can use more frequently occurring parts of the verb, will not lead to the automatic production which we are seeking.

It is important to remember that the drill is only a half-way stage in the learning process. Immediately after practising a verb in this way, opportunities should be given to practise in a realistic context.

Techniques worth exploring

TOTAL PHYSICAL RESPONSE

This is a technique whereby new words are presented with physical actions to be copied by the learners. Many people have found this a useful aid to memorising words and ensuring that they remain linked to their meanings. It is most appropriate for learning action verbs and in its simplest form it involves pupils obeying commands: 'Come in. Sit down. Go to the board. Write … Look … Listen …', etc.

Some teachers take the technique much further by doing regular exercise of verbs based on aerobics, using a musical background and combining verbs with other parts of speech: 'touch your knees', 'raise your arms', 'knock on the door', etc.

The idea can be further developed by adding actions to everything that is said. For example, a simple dialogue involving booking into a hotel may go like this:

Teacher:	*Bonjour, monsieur*	(teacher bows)
Pupils:	*Bonjour, madame*	(pupils bow)
Teacher:	*Vous désirez?*	(teacher draws a question mark in the air)
Pupils:	*Avez-vous une chambre, s'il vous plaît?*	(pupils hold up one finger, then put head on hands as for sleeping)
Teacher:	*Pour combien de personnes?*	(draws a question-mark in the air)
Pupils:	*Pour trois personnes*	(raise three fingers)
Teacher:	*Pour combien de nuits?*	(a rough sketch of a moon on the board and a question-mark)
Pupils:	*Pour trois nuits*	(three fingers and point at the moon)
Teacher:	*Avec douche ou baignoire?*	(points up to an imaginary shower and turns on the taps of the bath)
Pupils:		(copy whatever action is appropriate for the response)

When the dialogue has been practised as above, the class splits into pairs and practises in the same way. The next stage is to give each of the speakers a 'character' (a bad-tempered old hotel manager and bossy customer, perhaps). I have observed this sort of teaching with large classes of Year 10 boys who had been taught to take the matter quite seriously and clearly benefited from associating words with physical representations of them.

 ## DRAWING TIME

Some learners find it helpful to imagine time visually. The teacher may either point to his or her position in the room or draw on the board, to represent tenses:

This is sometimes further refined with squiggly lines for the imperfect and dots for the past definite, etc. Whenever adverbs of time are mentioned they are accompanied by pointing or drawing, according to the above sketch.

 ## LINKING WORDS

Another way of learning new words is to make a deliberate link between the target-language word and an English word which sounds or looks similar. This is a memory aid which has been supported by some serious research and with which a lot of learners feel comfortable. The system works best with concrete nouns and works like this:

The Spanish word for CAT is GATO
Imagine a CAT eating a lovely GATEAU

The Spanish for BEACH is PLAYA
Imagine you PLAY A game on the beach

The Spanish for DOOR is PUERTA
Imagine a hotel PORTER opening the door for you

These examples are quoted from Gruneberg's 'Linkword' series

The learners are asked to hold the pictures in their mind's eye for ten seconds before moving to the next word. Some schools have found this method remarkably successful, particularly with less able linguists.

THE POSSIBILITIES OF PROVERBS

In KS4 and above, a useful way of putting words into a memorable context is by learning proverbs or advertising jingles. Proverbs can be learned by pupils doing the following sorts of activity:

- matching up target-language proverbs with their English equivalents;
- matching up target-language proverbs with brief statements meaning the same;
- defining proverbs in their own words;
- telling (or writing) a story which illustrates the proverb.

There is a huge selection to choose from in all the major languages on the website **http:/perso. wanadoo.fr/proverbes**.

At KS3, a leisure activity or a holiday task might be something like this example:

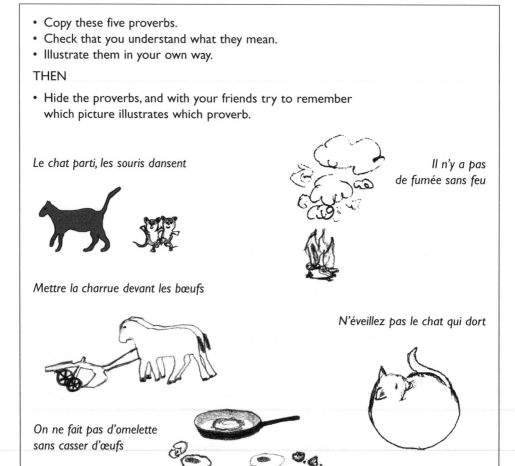

- Copy these five proverbs.
- Check that you understand what they mean.
- Illustrate them in your own way.

THEN

- Hide the proverbs, and with your friends try to remember which picture illustrates which proverb.

Le chat parti, les souris dansent

Il n'y a pas de fumée sans feu

Mettre la charrue devant les bœufs

N'éveillez pas le chat qui dort

On ne fait pas d'omelette sans casser d'œufs

The writing on the wall

What is on the wall can just be like wallpaper: it might brighten up the place but nobody ever looks at it. However, not only can it be beneficial to the pupils who prepare it, but it can also be used for vocabulary learning if the teacher remembers it is there! The following are some of the words on walls which have been seen on visits to schools and are pertinent to vocabulary acquisition:

- numbers 1–100 (the written forms of numbers do sometimes need to be **recognised**, although they are seldom needed for **reproduction**);
- days of the week and/or months of the year (a board with cut-outs into which pupils insert the day, date and month, at the beginning of each lesson);
- cut-outs of animals hanging from a beam (labelled in the target language);
- a washing-line hanging from a beam with cut-out articles of clothing (labelled);
- all the question forms in the target language;
- classroom 'survival' phrases which pupils always have to use;
- illustrated subjects from the timetable (symbols they have invented);
- '*Nos amis français*' – photographs of an exchange visit to the school with pictures of penfriends and their families, and places they have visited, etc… all labelled in the target language;
- '*Notre petit déjeuner français*' – obviously the day they put tablecloths on the school desks and brought in the coffee and *croissants!*
- '*On recherche …*' ('Rogues' gallery with descriptions in target language of the wanted criminals sometimes seen in DTP form);
- Coloured squares/balloons, etc with labels (handy to have on the wall whenever colours are needed);
- a blown-up map of the town, with symbols and labels in the target language;
- a map of the relevant country, so that towns and regions can be referred to when contexts are needed for new words.

8   Words and ICT

Effective vocabulary teaching is a question of:

* introducing new words in **a context**;
* gearing the context to the **needs** and **interests** of the learner;
* creating opportunities for **frequent practice**;
* making opportunities for learners to **encounter new words incidentally**.

Bearing this in mind it is worthwhile considering the value of technology in facilitating language acquisition.

VIDEO CAMERAS

The value of the camera (used sparingly) as a stimulus to learning vocabulary cannot be over-estimated. Great emphasis has been placed in this book on the importance of establishing appropriate **goals** for learners. It is highly desirable for these goals to be linked to real situations, which mainly depend on links with partners abroad (school, class, personal), but it is recognised that links take time to create and sometimes break in spite of people's best efforts. It is here that the video camera can be a good second-best. For young learners it will probably be sufficient to say that the goal at the end of a unit of work will be to make a five-minute video. (For example, learning the vocabulary for clothes can have as its goal a video of a mannequin parade. Learning food vocabulary can be given impetus by creating a series of advertisements for food as the goal.)

COMPUTERS

1   The most useful software on the computer from the point of view of language learning in general is still the **word processor**. The uses to which the word processor can be put have been detailed in various publications, such as InfoTech 2: *Text manipulation* (Hewer 1997) and New Pathfinder 3: *Impact on learning: What ICT can bring to MFL in KS3* (Dugard and Hewer 2003). What is worth reiterating here is that the importance of accuracy when the **written word** is being used can be given more point when a professional piece of work for display is the immediate goal. If a target-language spellchecker is available as well, the task becomes even more focused. When the goal of a particular unit of work depends upon written accuracy, older students might make use of the facilities of **PowerPoint** software to make presentations to their peers.

2   For pupils with their own computers, or post-16 students, an alternative (or addition) to keeping a vocabulary notebook is creating a personalised dictionary from the spelling section of the word-processing program. The value of sorting words into parts of speech has already been highlighted and the **custom dictionary** is an economical and efficient tool for doing this.

3   For older students, a **dictionary/thesaurus** in the target language on the computer is an invaluable addition to the more conventional reference works.

4   This is not the place to advertise the vast range of **CD-ROMs and databases** which have been designed specifically for language learning. All that need be said is that they can be a useful resource for giving learners the opportunity to encounter new words in a meaningful context. It is also worth considering what is available to young learners in the target-language countries, such as electronic encyclopedias and interactive DVDs. Many of these resources are also available on the Web.

5   The sorts of word-games outlined in Chapter 4, as well as more sophisticated versions of the same things, are available in an electronic form for use on the computer. *Fun With Texts, Storyboard, Developing Tray, TaskMagic*, etc are often popular with young learners. This sort of 'work' will merely be a waste of time if the teacher uses some of the ready-made packages which consist of words pupils will never need to **write**. If the texts are chosen to focus on what might be termed **key words for multi-purpose use** (that is the 'High-frequency words' of the *KS3 MFL Framework*) these text manipulation packages can be invaluable.

6   In Chapter 4: ('Playing games: a waste of time?') the value of getting pupils to make up their own word games was mentioned. Overleaf is an example of the sort of activity children enjoy if they have access to a computer.

Pupil instructions

When you have cracked the code, you can take some new words you have learned recently and convert them into a similar code. Make sure you don't make any spelling mistakes! You can then try them out on your friends.

If you have a computer, you might find that one of the fonts available on the word processor will provide the symbols for you. For example the code overleaf was made with the font called ZapfDingbats. You could also explore Windings or Webdings to make up your coded messages.

Did you get the words right?

RULE BRITANNIA – VIVA ESPAÑA – VIVE LA FRANCE – DEUTSCHLAND ÜBER ALLES

Here is the key. Can you work out the codes below?

A	B	C	D	E	F	G	H	I	J	K	L	M

N	O	P	Q	R	S	T	U	V	W	X	Y	Z

In English

En español

En français

Auf Deutsch

THE INTERNET

This is an area which may not have an obvious link with acquiring vocabulary. However, when the points which introduced this chapter are remembered it will be seen that the World Wide Web is a potentially rich source of up-to-date reading material. As was pointed out under 'Reading' (p79), the classrooms of today have become impoverished in this respect and where schools are linked to the Internet, a collection of suitable reading material can be downloaded for the purpose of creating a class 'library'. This will certainly take a certain amount of time on the part of the teacher, but in schools with post-16 learners there is a dual benefit to be gained from these students surfing the Net on the teacher's behalf. They will need to be directed to appropriate sites by the teacher in the first place, but selecting suitable material to be downloaded for use with younger pupils means that they themselves have to read it and that is a way of improving their own vocabulary.

The other potential of the Internet which is being used by some schools is for e-mail exchanges with partner schools in the target country. This is probably the most effective way of providing opportunities for frequent encounter of new vocabulary in an authentic context.

Behind the scenes, the teachers in both schools will need to suggest material which would be useful to their pupils. Topics which are to be studied in any particular term can then form the basis for e-mail letters (see InfoTech 7: *Communicating on-line* (Gläsmann 2004). The mechanics of surfing the Net are dealt with in InfoTech 3: *WWW/The Internet* (Atkinson 2002). Teachers of languages might well begin by using suitable search engines, such as **www.yahoo.fr**, **www.yahoo.de** and **www.yahoo.es**.

VIDEO-CONFERENCING

This is a fairly new area which has considerable potential as a tool for exposing pupils to a wide range of vocabulary in a real context. Schools which are lucky enough to have the appropriate facilities might be interested to look at work which has already been done such as in the Arbour Vale Special School in Slough. Here they have not only made contacts with Connecticut and France, but have even appointed teachers from South Africa after a 'tele-interview'.

For links to be successful, interested teachers will need to make contacts with like-minded teachers in the target-language school(s). As with traditional class-to-class or person-to-person links, the most fruitful contacts are those where the teachers concerned have done a certain amount of preparatory work (see *InfoTech 7*, mentioned above).

SATELLITE

TV programmes

The skills of listening and reading have already been identified as areas which it is vital for learners to develop if they are to increase their vocabulary acquisition. In addition to providing a library of reading and listening materials from traditional sources and from the Web, teachers now have access to the whole world of authentic television programmes.

Total language immersion may be possible only in the target-language country, but the availability of programmes by satellite can be a valuable substitute and, if well directed by the teacher, may even be better than total immersion, which can cause drowning! It is clearly not useful for a publication such as this to name particular programmes because of the ephemeral nature of television. However, it may be useful to suggest a few areas where teachers may find appropriate material.

For older learners there is clearly the whole gamut of news, documentaries and entertainment. For younger learners, the selection is more difficult because it is important not to swamp them. A search of what is currently available has produced the following types of programme which could well be used with younger learners:

- science education programmes designed for much younger children in France, Spain or Germany. The fact that our Key Stage 3 and 4 learners will be vaguely familiar with the experiments, along with visual support in the form of simple graphics, should aid comprehension;
- games programmes, where young people are quick to understand what is happening, even when there is not complete comprehension of the spoken word;
- animal and wildlife programmes with strong visual appeal;
- exploration and travel documentaries.

Using short TV programmes such as these can give pupils a sense of achievement: they may find that they can understand what is happening, even when the language is quite difficult. Giving learners the opportunity to hear genuine speech for purposes which are not patently didactic is a very important side of vocabulary acquisition. (See **www.wotsat.com/ tvlinks.html** for a listing of what is available and links to TV channels.)

Teletext

Most television channels have a Teletext which could be an ideal **reading** resource. There are areas here which the teacher could use for whole-class teaching or where individuals or small groups could be given specific reading tasks. The most obvious place to find this material is in the interest areas which are dearest to the hearts of the young person:

- the world of popular music (on some foreign language channels, there is information about groups, concerts, recordings, charts, etc);
- the world of sport (fixtures, league-tables, information about teams and players, etc.)

In addition to these two areas of interest, Televisión Español has under **Guía Joven** various sections which could be of interest and intelligible to younger learners:

- Turismo/Viajes: a series of information pages describing certain towns and regions;
- Discos: discos más vendidos;
- Pasatiempos;
- *Juegos ('Mensajes ocultos')*.

Another interesting section which should be accessible to quite elementary learners of Spanish is the topic of *Informática* itself. When discussing Information Technology, the key words are in English and furthermore, pupils will generally be vaguely familiar with the content of these pages. An ability to understand authentic language such as the following (and indeed the texts of which these are the headings) could be a valuable way of building confidence:

'El error de
los Pentium'

'Las tarjetas inteligentes: los
usuarios cargarón sus
tarjetas-chip 27.000 millones
de veces en un año ...'

'Estados Unidos busca nuevas
leyes para regular los daños
procedente del uso de
teclados y pantallas de
ordenador ...'

Introducción a Internet:
• Origen – desarrollo – internet en
  el mundo – ventajas y utilidad
• ¿Qué necesita para ...?
• A través de la voz ...
• Diccionario interno

In German, the Eurosport Deutsch channel Teletext pages are worth exploring for *News, Fussball* and *TV heute*.

Pupils have a genuine motivation to find out about these things and to compare information gleaned in this way with what they already know. The teacher's only problem may be to ensure that pupils keep in proportion the time spent on browsing the text!

The Teletext facility can also be used for more specific vocabulary practice. Take, for example, the departure and arrival times from Frankfurt airport. At the time of writing, these are available in French (TV5) or in German (Euronews).

Authentic material such as this can be used effectively to reinforce new vocabulary through repetitive questioning:

En français	Auf Deutsch
Départs	*Abfahrt*
A quelle heure part l'avion pour Londres?	Wann fliegt das Flugzeug in London?
Il part à 9 heures 25.	Es fliegt um 9.25 Uhr.
C'est bien 9 heures 25 du matin?	Ist das um 9.25 morgens?
Ah non, c'est 9 heures 25 du soir.	Nein, das ist 9.25 abends.
Il est à l'heure?	Landet es pünktlich?
Non, il a quinze minutes de retard.	Nein, es hat 15 Minuten Verspätung.
Arrivées	*Ankunft*
A quelle heure arrive l'avion de Paris?	Wann landet das Flugzeug in Amsterdam?
Il arrive à 20 heures 15.	Es landet um 20.15 Uhr.
Il est à l'heure?	Es hat eine halbe Stunde Verspätung.
Non, il a une demi-heure de retard.	
Also to practise the future: A quelle heure va partir … va arriver …?	
A quelle heure partira … arrivera …?	

Subtitles

Satellite TV offers another opportunity for learning vocabulary through absorption in the form of **subtitles**. There are two sorts of titles available from time to time:

- English or American films with target-language subtitles;
- target-language films or documentaries with subtitles in the target language (designed initially for deaf viewers). NB Subtitles are also available on all DVDs, with some offering foreign language subtitles, too.

Each of these facilities can be an invaluable way of absorbing new vocabulary at an intermediate to advanced level, although language learners do need a certain amount of training in disciplining themselves to read and listen at the same time.

Radio

While on the subject of the potential value of satellite, it should not be forgotten that radio programmes are also available by satellite and for advanced learners (and teachers wishing to keep up with what is happening in the world beyond the UK) the radio has always been an excellent source of information.

Depending on the area of the UK, the sound from long- or short-wave broadcasts can be poor to non-existent. The sound from satellite broadcasts, the Internet and on digital radio is perfect and there is a far wider choice than on conventional radio (see note on p82).

9 Language and cultural awareness

Particularly for the abler learners, though not exclusively the most advanced, it is a worthwhile exercise to get pupils to reflect occasionally on the reasons why they all have to study a language within the National Curriculum. In this way, they may come to understand that communicative competence for some imaginary future use is not the only, or even the most significant reason for this requirement. There will be occasions in teaching a language (a whole lesson or a part of a lesson) when teachers will wish to focus specifically on some aspect of vocabulary for its own sake, without gearing it to any particular communicative objective. In this chapter we will consider some of the possibilities.

LANGUAGE AWARENESS

It is not long ago that what was being advocated by some people was a general programme of language awareness before pupils embarked upon a particular foreign language. Although language awareness was mentioned in the National Curriculum as one of the principle aims of language teaching, we reached the stage when heightening pupils' awareness of language was minimalised in the MFL classroom. The *KS3 MFL Framework* again focuses on some aspects of language awareness under 'Words' and 'Sentences'.

Where do words come from?

New words for new worlds: Coining

English		Français	
mini-skirt	track-suit	la navette	un baladeur
trainers	shell-suit	une croissanterie	une jardinerie
telephone	television	une grillerie	une droguerie
micro-chip	mouse	un aéroglisseur	les puces
hardware	software	les bébés éprouvettes	une souris
test-tube babies	pacemakers	le must	le look
compact discs	body-building	un video-clip	un spot publicitaire
		les stimulateurs-cardiaques	

New words for new worlds: Borrowing

English	Deutsch	Español	Français
From French:	**From English:**	**From English:**	**From English:**
restaurant	der Computer	el coca-cola light	le camping
soup	der Jogging	el waterpolo	le caravaning
menu	die Hardware	un hooligan	le shampooing
salmon	die Software	la jet-set	le parking
beef	die CD	**From Arabic:**	le smoking
mutton	die Cassette	una almohada	un snack
pork	die Stereo	un azulejo	un self
architecture	die Hifi	el azafrán	une hi-fi
government	die Rock Musik		un talkie-walkie
justice	die Maschine		un walkman
administration	das Internet		le far-west
art	das Keyboard		le body-building
science	die Jeans		un docker
cassette	der Manager		le cake
disco	der Boss		**From other languages:**
	das Business		un toréador
			un fjord
			une geisha
			une guérilla
			un cappuccino

New words for new worlds: Proper names (people and places)

English	Deutsch	Español	Français
Hoover	ein Tempo	un minipimer (*hand mixer*)	une poubelle
Kleenex	Selter	un suizo (*teacake*)	une guillotine
Sandwich	Hansaplast	el delco (*distributor*)	l'eau de Javel
to send someone to Coventry	Frankfurter	una veronica (*bull-fighting pass*)	une montgolfière
	Berliner	el cárter (*crank-case*)	un judas
	der Kaba		une colonne Morris
	ein Judas		un apollon
			le champagne (*from* La Champagne)
			le bordeaux
			un Perrier
			limoger quelqu'un

It can be a useful exercise for teachers to consult with their English language colleagues about areas where language awareness can best be raised in the MFL classroom.

To deal with the above issues **in English** will mean that pupils can more easily make connections with their own language and see the ways in which vocabulary expands in roughly the same way in all languages. It is suggested that in each case the starting point should be the English word, demonstrating the particular phenomenon of derivations. From here it is a natural step to move on to derivations of a similar sort in the target language.

The vocabulary of new technology itself can make an interesting study for teachers and more advanced learners. In France, a state commission for the promotion of Gallic technology and business jargon has decreed that *'le courriel'* should replace *'le mail'*. Whether this new coinage (from *'courrier électronique'*) will actually stick depends on the relative strengths of the principles of ease of use versus national pride! The following lists make an interesting starting point and can be developed as new words are coined and old words disappear.

Ease of use versus national pride

French ICT terms which have not stuck	
la toile	*the Web*
le courriel	*e-mail*
l'arrosage	*spam*
incendier	*to burn*
une causette	*chat*
le gestionnaire de périphérique	*driver*
un fouineur	*hacker*
une frimousse	*smiley*
un logiciel de navigation	*browser*
la diffusion systématique sur la toile	*webcasting*
un numériseur	*scanner*
la souris	*mouse*

French ICT terms which have stuck	
un ordinateur	*computer*
numérique	*digital*
l'informatique	*ICT*
le logiciel	*software*
télécharger	*to download*
une puce	*chip*
une bogue	*bug*
un agenda électronique	*personal organiser*
un site	*website*
amorcer	*to boot*
une fenêtre	*window*
planter	*to crash*
un moteur de recherche	*search engine*

The vocabulary of slang can be an interesting topic for an occasional lesson at any stage beyond complete beginners. The following lists might serve as starters:

Words with a curiosity value

Slang and 'lazy words'

English	Deutsch	Español	Français
Let the pupils provide their own ideas but include:	joggen, joben	hacer el canguro *(to baby-sit)*	chouette
thingy	gemanaged	hacer el tonto *(to act the fool)*	extra
thingummy	Was geht?	somos todos oídos *(we're all ears)*	terrible
whatsits	Er hat nicht alle Tassen im Schrank	ir por su aire *(to do one's own thing)*	génial
	abgespaced	un chisme	le petit coin
	einsame Spike		T'as pigé?
	klasse, genial		le toubib
	die Kohle, verknallt		T'es dingue, toi!
	schrill		un mec
	pennen		mon frangin/ ma frangine
	dingsda, dingsbums, dasda		une patate
			le resto
			métro, boulot, dodo
			un truc/un machin/ un bidule

The sound of words

A key between oracy and literacy is a firm grasp of phoneme to grapheme correspondence. Within this context, any time spent on training of the ear and focused on the sound of words is time well spent. There are four main reasons for doing this:

- most learners enjoy singing or speaking aloud, so long as they are not alone;
- natural shyness (particularly in the middle years of mixed-gender classes) can be overcome by speaking together with others;

- concentrating on perfect copying of a native speaker helps the learner to realise that the speech organs have to move differently in each language;
- the 'feel' of making foreign sounds becomes familiar to the learner.

Songs

The first type of sound practice is the song. This is an area which has been covered comprehensively in Classic Pathfinder 3: *Inspiring performance*. It is sufficient here to emphasise how useful a specially constructed song can be in the context of vocabulary learning. The use of songs for vocabulary reinforcement offers an opportunity for swift and painless repetition practice, and the benefits of total physical response (see Chapter 7) will be added when gestures can be included with the songs.

The pronunciation list

In any language, a pronunciation list is occasionally useful for the four reasons mentioned above. In French particularly, the pronunciation list has the additional purpose of drawing attention to the various possible **spellings** of different sounds. The example which appears opposite has been used at intermediate to advanced levels, but simpler lists can be constructed to meet the needs of different levels. Pupils can be trained to make their own pronunciation lists, giving them another opportunity for involvement in the process of learning.

Tongue-twisters

A third way of concentrating on the sound of words is by the use of the tongue-twister. Sometimes, this may be a way of tackling a particular sound which learners are finding difficult. At other times, a tongue twister may simply serve as a good warm-up device for the beginning of the lesson. The examples on pp104–105 have been found to work particularly well in the classroom but teachers may be interested to follow up others which can be found on the website **www.uebersetzung.at/twister/index.htm**.

a	J'ai marqué le résult**at** de mes ach**ats** dans mon agend**a**. Ils sont adéqu**ats**
ail	Les dét**ails** du b**ail** donnent du trav**ail**
euil	Du s**euil**, je vois mon portef**euille** dans le faut**euil**
eille	Je surv**eille** les ab**eilles** qui s'év**eillent** dans la corb**eille**
ain / in	Le méde**cin** prend le tr**ain** d'Am**iens** après-dem**ain** pour aller à Berl**in**
un	Chac**un** veut un empr**unt** au moment opport**un**. C'est comm**un**!
ame	Les télégr**ammes** pour mad**ame** viennent const**amm**ent d'une sage-f**emme**
an / en	Les cli**ents** du march**and** de g**ants** sont exig**eants**
è / ais	Je f**ais** expr**ès** d'avoir des fr**ais** au mois de m**ai**
é	L'employ**é** d**é**vou**é** sera r**é**compens**é**
eu	Les y**eux** de mon nev**eu** sont pleins de f**eu**
eur	Le chauff**eur** de l'ambassad**eur** chante de tout c**œur** en graissant le mot**eur**
au / o / eau	Les **o**s de mon d**os** sont en morc**eaux**
eu / au / eau	Les chev**eux** et les chev**aux** de mon nev**eu** sont b**eaux**
	Mon premier nev**eu** habite à Fontainebl**eau**
	Mon deuxième nev**eu** habite à Montr**eux**
oi	Les villag**eois** dans le b**ois** mangent des p**ois** avec les d**oigts**
	Il y avait une f**ois** un marchand de f**oie** qui vendait son f**oie** dans la ville de F**oix**
oin	J'ai bes**oin** d'un tém**oin** de l'accident du rond-p**oint**
oir	Si j'ai bonne mém**oire**, l'arm**oire** provis**oire** est dans le laborat**oire** près du mir**oir**
on / om	Les n**oms** et prén**oms** de mes compagn**ons** sont l**ongs**
onne	La patr**onne** a téléph**oné**. Il n'y a pers**onne**? Ça m'ét**onne**!
ou	Le voy**ou** à gen**oux** dans le tr**ou** plein de caill**oux** mange des ch**oux**
our	Tous les j**ours** au carref**our** du faub**ourg**, le s**ourd** fait des disc**ours**
u	L'instit**ut** ten**u** par Monsieur Cam**us** est très conn**u**
ui	Les fr**uits** c**uits** sont grat**uits** aujourd'**hui**
c + a / o / u	**C**oco a acheté le **c**adeau pour **C**arole
c + e / i / y	**C**écile et **C**yrille sont **c**ertainement i**c**i
g + a / o / u	**G**uy, le **g**orille, **g**onfle sa **g**rande **g**orge
g + e / i	**G**eorges joue **g**énéralement avec **G**igi

Des phrases à déchirer la mâchoire

- Avez-vous vu la lune au-dessus des dunes?
- Ce chat chauve caché sous six souches de sauge sèche
- Dis donc, Zoë, tu sais qu'il y a eu soixante-cinq concerts super-chers à Buenos-Aires, dont six au laser?
- Je pense que je peux – je pense que je peux – je pense que je peux …
- Les chaussettes de l'archiduchesse, sont-elles sèches ou archi-sèches?
- Ma bague – ma bague – Ma bague – ma bague – Ma bague …
- Mon chat, Pompon, monte sur le rayon où nous gardons la confiture de melon, les oignons et les concombres
- Mon frère, Gaston, tombe souvent et rompt les boutons de son bon veston
- Mon oncle Léon ronfle longtemps dans sa chaise longue
- Panier – piano – panier – piano – panier – piano …
- Si six scies scient six saucissons, six cent six scies scient six cent six saucissons
- Tonton, ton thé t'a-t-il ôté ta toux?
- Toto le titi voit le tutu chez tata
- Un chasseur sachant sacher sans son chien doit savoir chasser sans son chien

Zungenbrecher

- Der Potsdamer Postkutscher putzt den Potsdamer Postkutschwagen
- Die böse Baronin von Fleetchen schikanierte das Gretchen, ihr Mädchen, bis ein schöner Prinz kam und Gretchen zur Frau nahm. Jetz putzt Frau von Fleetchen bei Gretchen.
- Es spricht die Frau von Rubinstein: Mein Hund, der ist nicht stubenrein
- Blaukraut bleibt Blaukraut und Brautkleid bleibt Brautkleid
- In Ulm, um Ulm und um Ulm herum
- Kleine Kinder können keine Kirschkerne knacken
- Klemens Klasse kitzelt Klaras kleines Kind
- Tausend Tropfen tröpfeln traurig, traurig tröpfeln tausend Tropfen. Tip, tip, tup!
- Trink keinen Rum, denn Rum macht dumm
- Viele Fliegen fliegen vielen Fliegen nach
- Wir Wiener Waschweiber würden weiße Wäsche waschen, wenn wir warmes, weiches Wasser hätten
- Zehn Zähne zieht mir der Zahnarzt im Dezember
- Zehn Ziegen zogen zehn Zentner Zucker zum Zoo

- Balbina vive en Valencia, Viviano vive en Bilbao
- El cielo está enladrillado. ¿Quién lo desenladrillará?
  El desenladrillador que lo desenladrille, buen desenladrillador será
- El jamón que vende Gerónimo en el bar Gijón es famoso en Geron
- El perro de San Roque no tiene rabo, ¿por qué?
  Porque Ramón se lo ha robado
- ¿Más más que menos o más menos que más?
- Once cervezas y doce zumos de naranja. Gracias.
- Un triste tigre comía trigo en un trigal
  Dos tristes tigres comían trigo en un trigal
  Tres tristes tigres comían trigo en un trigal

Intonation practice

Words which even quite young learners can appreciate are those which bear no meaning, but are extremely common in normal native speech. Occasionally, the teacher may wish to concentrate on those typical phrases used by native speakers which bear no 'meaning' but which express:

- hesitation;
- being unable to find the right word;
- strong **feelings**.

They are also useful communication strategies, giving you time to think (see Part 1, p48).

A little choral imitation practice, with special attention being paid to **intonation** is a good way of shaking off inhibitions about speaking which adolescents sometimes develop. If recordings of this sort of thing can be found, they can be most useful. Alternatively, it requires some acting ability on the part of the teacher:

English	Deutsch	Español	Français
… Ummm …	Ach so! Ohwey!	estee …	… euh …
Garn! Gerraway!	Ja! Los!	a ver…	Mais, non!
Why no, man!	Na, so was!	Bueno …	Oh là là là là là!
Naah!	Ach wo! Wie bitte?	¡Ojalá!	Zut alors!
… you know	Blöd!		Tu penses!
… look you!	Meinst du?		J'en ai marre!

THE CULTURAL DIMENSION OF VOCABULARY

The cultural dimension of vocabulary study is an area which teachers may wish to explore with their pupils from time to time.

The Harris Report, which preceded the National Curriculum, pointed out that without a growing awareness of the **culture** of the target-language speakers, 'comprehension of **even basic words** may be partial or approximate'. What is meant by the cultural content of words is the connotations that words have for a particular group of people. It is by exploring these connotations that pupils can begin to appreciate the cultural aspect of vocabulary.

There are three main approaches to teaching pupils how to investigate connotations and to compare them with what appear to be the same words in their own language.

Word associations

English pupils are asked to write down in a 'spidergram' or 'mind map' all that comes into their minds when they hear or see particular words. They then compare their mind maps with each other and then do a further investigation by looking up the definitions of the words in a bilingual dictionary. Target-language pupils do the same with the 'equivalent' words, the results are exchanged and a comparative study is made, looking at the words in a variety of contexts.

The words which were used as examples for the post-16 students were 'private' and 'public'/'*privat*' and '*öffentlich*'. At a slightly lower level, such words as the following might be appropriate words to explore in the same way:

English	Deutsch	Español	Français
cheese	queso	fromage	Käse
bread	pan	pain	Brot
family	familia	famille	Familie
school	colegio	école	Schule

Asking and listening

Two other ways of sensitising pupils to the cultural aspect of vocabulary are:

- organising a series of short interviews with individuals in the target language (e.g. the members of a visiting school trip) in which the questions are designed in such a way as to find out what connotation any word has for them. For instance, one of the questions might be: 'Tell me about your family'. This would be seen to produce different results from different sets of speakers, according to how wide their 'family' was considered in their culture.
- conducting a group interview in the target language (perhaps half a dozen from the same visiting school) where they discuss particular words and what they mean to them. The leader of the discussion might start with a leading question such as: 'What do you understand by the word "work"?'.

In both cases, notes would be taken and compared with similar questions asked in English to the 'home team'.

Corpus linguistics

The technique of this field of study is to build very large data banks of words in their contexts. The data in the Bank of English, for example, is composed of approximately 42 million words from written texts and fourteen million words of transcribed speech. These data banks are compiled by analysing both written texts and transcribed speech. Words from the Bank of English can be looked up on the Internet at **www.cobuild.collins.co.uk** and new Collins dictionaries are now based on this corpus. When a word is looked up it is quoted with a few words to each side and a perusal of these phrase groups helps the learner to appreciate the contexts and associations of the words. The illustration overleaf (Figure 4) is drawn from the 40 lines displayed when the word 'morning' is looked up.

Although these databases are used mainly by linguists, teachers, translators and advanced students, it is a fascinating way of getting to the meaning beneath the surface of words. In schools, advanced learners could find this a useful way of investigating the essence of words and making their own collection of common words in context as in Figure 4. Even KS3 learners could be sensitised to the concept of words in context by studying an example such as the above in English, and the importance of learning the *KS3 MFL Framework* 'High-frequency words' in context.

Figure 4

Did you fax them yesterday	morning?	It was directly after I …
Hi. Good	morning.	Have you got any wrapping paper?
When we were talking this	morning,	John mentioned that …
There's fresh controversy this	morning,	about the sinking of the Scottish …
How long are they here in the	morning?	About half an hour or so.
He took a walk before breakfast each	morning	and again in the evening.
She wakes us up in the	morning	and makes something to eat.
On Friday	morning	at 5am he telephoned the radio studio.
He promised to talk to Sharon in the	morning	at school. After he had gone, she…
Last Saturday	morning,	I was so shocked that I …
It never really matches that early	morning	cup of freshly-ground coffee.
With official car parks full by mid-	morning	desperate drivers have been known to …
because he didn't have a fridge. One	morning	I got up at about 4am and went and …
As soon as I get home, late tomorrow	morning,	I think I will …
… will make sure your child enjoys a	morning	in our care.
… will be announced on Thursday	morning	in Los Angeles.
Her comments on Good	Morning	Scotland seemed lucid.
… producing their malty	morning	tea in enormous volumes.
… after it was stopped yesterday	morning.	The tanker was …
… the failure of their mission. This	morning	the attack on Serbia …
… moved in the half-darkness of early	morning	toward the lip of …
In the	morning,	we headed south …
Well not at half-past six in the	morning	we can't. You're …
… and would arrive early this	morning	when another effort …
The audience for Good	Morning,	which Anne co-presents …

10 Helping pupils to help themselves

An aspect of teaching which is easy to forget is telling pupils **why** they are doing things, letting them into the secrets. Learners of every age need to have confidence that their teachers know what they are doing and telling them the reasons why they are doing particular activities (a particular homework or test, the reason for playing a game, etc) can be a motivating factor in their learning.

It may be worth considering giving them an occasional hand-out as a way of focusing their attention on matters which it can be too easily assumed that they know. Figures 5 and 6 are suggestions for the form that tips for studying might take. You might find it useful to look at the checklist of strategies in Part 1 for some more ideas.

In Classic Pathfinder 2: *Challenging classes,* Jenifer Alison explores ways of motivating challenging classes. It can be argued that the principles she outlines can be applied to teaching at any level. The use of 'Tips of the day' is a practical way of demonstrating to pupils that:

- they have our trust and respect;
- they are valued;
- they have a chance to participate in their own learning;
- they can feel safe and not embarrassed.

In a class plenary after a 'tip' has been acted upon, pupils can discuss whether or not the advice has worked for them, how it could be improved, whether it should be rewritten for future pupils, etc. These are ways of helping pupils to see a point in what they are asked to do.

Homework	• Organise your evening into what you **have** to do and what you **want** to do • Make a quick timetable (don't forget to include your favourite TV programme or that game of football) • If your homework includes **learning,** put it into three ten-minutes slots, rather than one half hour • sit at a desk or table • give yourself a time limit • start with the hard things first • leave the music until you have a break in your work
Testing each other	• Spend a couple of minutes looking through the words to be tested • Get your partner to hide his or her list • Ask for the word in the way the teacher tells you • If the answer doesn't come immediately, supply the word and move on • After several more words, go back to the one he or she didn't know • and ask again **Stop** • Change roles **If you work quickly you will learn quickly and it can be fun!**
Reading or listening	• When we are learning a new language it has been discovered that the best way to enlarge your vocabulary is to read widely and listen to lots of people talking • What you have been given for homework should be interesting or enjoyable (or both!) • If you don't think it is, do it just the same. **Remember: this is the best way to build up enough new words to be able to understand this language.**

Reading	• Glance quickly through the text, to try to work out what it's about (if there's a title, there'll probably be a clue or two in it) • Read fairly quickly, but pause at full stops to check that you have the meaning (if not, read that bit again) • At the end, read the whole text again • If there are words that are still puzzling you at this stage, look them up in the dictionary **Resist the temptation to look up words you don't know too soon!**
Learning a list of words by heart	• Split the list into groups of three or four words • Learn each group separately • Test yourself (each group at a time) – be tough! • Test the whole list • Do something totally different • Test yourself again (mark those that you don't get right) • Do something else • Test yourself again • Get someone else to test you • Then, test someone else yourself, trying to rely on your memory to check whether they are right
Speaking homework	• In class tomorrow you will be asked to give sentences, using each of the new words in your list • Don't write anything down • Think of your sentence • If you don't know how to say something, try to put it another way (don't be too ambitious) • If you really need a particular word that you don't know, look it up in the dictionary • Record your sentence • Listen to it and record it again if you're not satisfied • Now do the same with the other words in your list
Pairwork	• When you are working in pairs, everyone in the class can practise at the same time • For pairwork to be useful you must start as soon as the teacher says: *'Bon, travaillez à deux'* (or other target-language command) • You need to work quietly and quickly • You will have a very short time limit, so you need to get started straight away • As soon as you hear *'Bon, arrêtez'* (or other target-language command) stop working with your partner and be prepared to work as a whole class again

Using post-16 learners

The value of using pupils to create word games for each other has already been mentioned. Using older learners to create materials for more junior pupils is also useful for both age groups.

Even when schools do not have their own sixth form they are usually connected to a post-16 institution. In the first few weeks of the post-GCSE course, one of the ways of 'bridging the gap' is to take the Areas of Experience C, D and E and study them from a more mature point of view. This is also the time when teachers need to make sure that advanced learners have the tools they will need (dictionary skills, knowledge of basic grammatical terminology, etc).

It is during this period that a valid language task is for students to examine the vocabulary list for a particular topic in a junior coursebook and compare it with what is needed to achieve the specific goal set by the teacher. For example, they are shown the section in Chapter 1 on 'Weather'. They are asked to select key words for that task and list them according to the different parts of speech, saying whether they will be needed for receptive or productive use (another useful concept for them to think about at this stage). In this way, they are revising their own basic vocabulary and at the same time beginning to look at vocabulary analytically. In the process, they are ensuring that their grammatical terminology is in place. The result of this 'research' can then be used as the basis for vocabulary lists for younger learners, thus killing two birds with one stone.

The problem of finding sufficient continuous reading material for junior pupils can also be partly solved by asking for some creative writing from older students. They can be given a list of words from a specific part of a junior course and asked to weave a story round it. Alternatively, good material has sometimes come from giving older students a free rein.

The main thrust of this part of the book has been to emphasise that the most effective and permanent vocabulary learning is the result of frequent exposure to a wide range of spoken and written language, supported by plenty of oral and written practice of an enjoyable and interesting kind. The most successful language learners are those who are not only motivated by the need to pass examinations but are also stimulated by imaginative and creative teaching and materials.

Appendix A:
Groupwork and pairwork

Frequent mention of pairwork has been made in both parts of the book. Since recent observation suggests that there is a tendency to abandon this mode of working, it is worth considering the reasons why it does not always work as well as it might.

The following disadvantages of **groupwork** are good reasons for using it only occasionally in highly controlled situations:

- it is an invitation to waste time talking about other things;
- it creates an opportunity for disruptive behaviour;
- most classrooms are too small for adequate privacy between groups;
- it involves moving furniture;
- the more retiring pupils are not involved.

On the other hand, with **pairwork** it is much easier to overcome these problems and, provided certain principles are followed, the advantages are worth the effort. Pupils need a certain amount of training to go into the **pairwork mode** at frequent intervals during a lesson. It should not be seen as a special event, needing a lot of disruption.

To begin with, they might be given a slip of paper with 'The tip of the day' to study (see Chapter 10). Then the teacher needs to give the class several practice runs when everyone is thinking about **getting the system working**, rather than worrying about what they are actually learning.

Pupils need training to go into the pairwork mode at frequent intervals during a lesson. It should not be seen as a special occasion, needing a lot of organisation.

They need a certain amount of initial training, when the procedure will be more important than the content. They need practice in these matters:

- being quiet and business-like;
- working quickly;
- talking in the target language all the time;
- moving on to another task if they finish early;
- moving back to the **whole-class** mode immediately they are told.

The teacher needs to:

- set the task as briefly as possible, demonstrating with the help of a pupil rather than talking, and ignoring questions at this stage;
- give them a time limit (two or three minutes is often ample);
- watch to check that they begin immediately, quietly naming those who do not do so;
- answer individual questions;
- avoid the temptation to get too involved with individuals;
- continue to watch;
- supply an extra task for those who finish early.

Once classes are trained to work co-operatively in quick bursts of pairwork like this, it will be found that it is an excellent strategy for vocabulary learning and reinforcement.

Appendix B:
Creating your own listening materials

One of the ways of doing this is by using a Foreign Language Assistant, or a group of Assistants. It is unlikely that overseas students will have done anything like this before, so it is worthwhile spending a little time before they start on a training workshop. Before a recording session, the teacher will draw their attention to a few important points and then they will make some practice recordings. In this way, the teacher will acquire material which will be really useful and of lasting worth.

- The end product should sound **natural** and **unrehearsed**.
- Think about the **level** of the learner (e.g. KS3 or KS4).
- Plan first in your mind. **Avoid the temptation to write** (unless you want to jot down a few key words).

Material produced by the Assistant(s) may be in the form of monologues, dialogues or discussions. Figures 7–8 are suggestions about the sorts of things they can talk about, without too much difficulty. Recordings such as these will provide a rich source of material for classroom use and will be a way of building up a bank of material suitable for listening homework.

Another useful technique for collecting sound records is the interview with anybody who is available. Friends and acquaintances abroad can be pressed into service for this, or a group of exchange pupils can be taken to one side for a quick recording session. If this is a technique which teachers have not yet exploited, a few hints may be useful (see Figure 9, overleaf).

Material collected in the ways described below may sometimes be used for classroom presentation of new vocabulary, but it is more likely to produce material for **gist listening**, which can be recorded (on cassette, CD or DVD) and lent out for homework. It can also be placed in a listening library with self-access during 'quiet reading/listening' periods. If it is handled in this way, there does need to be some check that work set has been done, but it does not have to take the form of a written test with questions and answers! By asking pupils just to tell you and the class about the content of a recording, they are learning to use new vocabulary for a **purpose** and incidentally reinforcing it. Teachers who have been able to find time to organise regular listening of this kind have been able to perceive a marked improvement in vocabulary acquisition.

Figure 7

monologues

1 Talk about where you live in your home country/in England (house/flat … old/new … where … number of bedrooms … other rooms … where you spend most of the time: indoors/garden/balcony, etc).

2 Talk about what you can/can't do (speak Italian … play the piano … use a computer … speak Japanese … type … swim … play tennis … ski … cook … draw, etc).

3 Talk about what other members of your family can/can't do (see list under **2**).

4 Talk about what you/your family like doing in your spare time. (What you/they would do if you/they won the lottery.)

5 A short history of your life.

6 What you have found different about your home town and where you live now. What you have found different about your own country and England. (Don't be frightened about mentioning negative reactions as well as positive reactions. Say what you find odd/unusual/surprising/ annoying.)

7 What you are going to do at Christmas/in the summer/during the next holidays. What you are going to do this weekend/next year, etc. And members of your family?

8 What you did during your last holiday/last weekend, etc.

9 What it was like when your grandparents were young.

Figure 8

dialogues & discussions

Two or three native speakers get together and:

1 decide on the objective (where it will fit into the Scheme of Work);

2 look at the available vocabulary (perhaps by consulting a GCSE list of vocabulary);

3 produce a scenario (Where are you? … Who are you …? What are you discussing? … Who will take what angle?);

4 don't write anything down;

5 don't worry about slips of the tongue (that's the advantage of not using professional actors).

Figure 9

interviews

1 The interviewer should jot down a few key words and question forms (NB If he or she writes down a whole series of questions it is unlikely that the result will sound natural and unrehearsed).

2 Think of questions which will encourage the other person to speak:
not 'Do you …', 'Are you …', 'Have you', etc.
but 'Tell me about …', 'Why …?', What was it like …?

3 Think of the use to which you hope to put the recording:
• for reinforcement of vocabulary, previously presented;
• for the presentation of new vocabulary;
• for practising the use of specific tenses (future, past, conditional);
• for providing opportunities for extending vocabulary;
• for cultural awareness (differences, similarities).

References

Atkinson, T. (2002) InfoTech 3: *WWW/The Internet.* 2nd ed. CILT.

Department for Education and Skills (2003) *Key Stage 3 National Strategy. Framework for teaching Modern Foreign Languages: Years 7, 8 and 9.* HMSO.

Dugard, C. and Hewer, S. (2003) New Pathfinder 3: *Impact on learning: What ICT can bring to MFL in KS3.* CILT.

Gläsmann, S. (2004) InfoTech 7: *Communicating on-line.* CILT.

Hamilton, J., McLeod, A. and Fawkes, S. (2003) Classic Pathfinder 3: *Inspiring performance: Focus on drama and song.* CILT.

Hewer, S. (1997) InfoTech 2: *Text manipulation.* CILT.

Jones, B., Halliwell, S. and Holmes, B. (2002) Classic Pathfinder 1: *You speak, they speak: Focus on target language use.* CILT.

The Open University (2002) ILIAD (International Languages Inservice at a Distance) CD-ROM. The Open University.

FURTHER READING

Hatch, E. and Brown, C. (1995) *Vocabulary, semantics and language education.* Cambridge University Press.

> A comprehensive textbook prepared for an introductory course in Linguistics at the University of California. In addition to a complete study of the theories and research there are many practical suggestions for students of English.

Gruneberg, M. M. (1994) *Spanish/French by association.* NTC Publishing.

> Two of a series of Linkword books in various languages which develop the notion of learning vocabulary through association with similar-sounding English words.

Lewis, M. (1999) *How to study foreign languages.* Macmillan.

> Written for students studying a language in senior secondary schools or as part of a university degree. Part 2: 'Strategies for language acquisition' (Chapter 7) starts with 'Vocabulary learning'.

McCarthy, M. (1990) *Vocabulary.* Oxford University Press.

> A manual for teachers of English as a second language. Considers theoretical, descriptive and psycholinguistic models of the English vocabulary. It then offers many tasks for the teacher, designed to explore ways of translating theory into practice. Much of it is applicable to MFL.

Nation, P. (ed) (1990) *New ways in teaching vocabulary.* Alexandria, USA: Teachers of English to Speakers of Other Languages.

> A TESOL handbook with contributions from teachers of English around the world. The activities are soundly based on well-tried principles. Many of the ideas are adaptable to MFL teaching.

Schmitt, N. (2000) *Vocabulary in language teaching.* Cambridge University Press.

> An applied linguistic text for teachers. See particularly Chapters 7–9.

Wenden, A. and Ruben, J. (1987) *Learner strategies in language learning.* Prentice-Hall International.

> A collection of contributions from teacher trainers and applied linguists on various aspects of language learning. There are interesting chapters on mnemonic techniques for learning vocabulary and promoting learner autonomy.

timeless topics for all MFL teachers

Classic Pathfinders deal with those MFL issues that will never go away. Based on the wisdom contained in the best-selling titles in the *Pathfinder* series, the material has been re-written and updated by the original authors in the light of the challenges of today's classroom. Each title contains re-editions of two related titles in the *Pathfinder* range which are truly 'classic'.

Classic Pathfinder 1

You speak, they speak: focus on target language use

Barry Jones, Susan Halliwell and Bernardette Holmes

Classic Pathfinder 2

Challenging classes: focus on pupil behaviour

Jenifer Alison and Susan Halliwell

Classic Pathfinder 3

Inspiring performance: focus on drama and song

Judith Hamilton, Anne McLeod and Steven Fawkes

Classic Pathfinder 4

Doing it for themselves: focus on learning strategies and vocabulary building

Vee Harris and David Snow

classic pathfinder

the MFL perspective on today's issues

new pathfinder

New Pathfinders

provide an expert MFL perspective on national initiatives. They are designed to support the language-teaching profession by ensuring that MFL has its own voice and ideas on the issues in education today.

New Pathfinders provide user-friendly support, advice and reference material for today's CPD agenda.

New Pathfinder 1

Raising the standard: Addressing the needs of gifted and talented pupils

Anneli McLachlan

New Pathfinder 2

The language of success: Improving grades at GCSE

Dave Carter

New Pathfinder 3

Impact on learning: What ICT can bring to MFL in KS3

Claire Dugard and Sue Hewer

New Pathfinder 4

It makes you think!: Creating engagement, offering challenges

Barry Jones and Ann Swarbrick